M000191965

The Science and Secrets Behind Seven Words That Motivate, Engage, and Influence

MAGIC WORDS

TIM DAVID

MAGIC WORDS: The Science and Secrets Behind Seven Words that Motivate, Engage, and Influence (Penguin Random House)

"Elegant and concise."

—*NY Times*

"Top ten psychology book of 2016."

—*Blinkist Magazine*

Fans of Dr. Robert Cialdini, Daniel Pink, and Malcolm Gladwell will enjoy this in-depth look at the often surprising magic behind how words can inspire and influence others. By exploring seven "magic words," Tim David explains the important psychology behind how what we say affects those around us in business and in life. Full of startling scientific research, humorous anecdotes, and word-for-word scripts, this book will help you be a better leader, salesperson, or parent.

Available now at: **www.MagicWordsBook.com** and all major book retailers.

AVAILABLE NOW FOR FREE

FLIP

The **Four Levels** of Influencing People

TIM DAVID

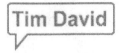

FLIP: The Four Levels of Influencing People

Published by Tim David
Lakeville, MA, United States

ISBN: 978-0-9996297-0-3
First edition: January 2019

To nice flower guy.

CONTENTS

Introduction: Flipping Influence 1

Technique
The School that Words Built 19
The Splinter of the Century 27
The Vegetable War 31
How to Generate Sudden Interest in Old Ideas 37
How to Ask for Something in an Email 41
Writing a Persuasive Speech—The ACA Formula 49
The Elevator Pitch for Your Elevator Pitch 55
A Sneaky Trick for When They Tune You Out 61
Then, Now, How: The Power Story Formula 65
The Cootie Whisperer 69
Three Words that Could Save Your Business (Or Your Life) 73

Relationship
The American Who Hijacked the Bus 81
The Tiny but Huge Difference Between Communication and Connection 87
Overheard at the Gym 91
The Bad Job Interview and The Idiot Salesman 97
The Best Emotion for Any Interaction 101
Do You Come Across as Confident or Cocky? 105

Understanding
When Other People Stress You Out 111

Revenge of the Words 123

A "Remote Control" for Brains? 127

Why Nobody Listens to You 131

Influence in the Bathroom 135

The Most Famous Sentence in the History of Influence 143

Ethics

Without This, You're not Even in the Game 149

The Anti-Godfather Maneuver—Make an Offer They CAN Refuse 151

"Be as Calculating as you are Genuine..." 159

Be an Advocate for Their Future Selves 165

Child Abuse or Father of the Year? 171

Nice Chapters Finish Last 175

Become More Influential: Your Next Step 187

Acknowledgements 191

INTRODUCTION: FLIPPING INFLUENCE

In high school, my biggest dream in life was to be a professional magician. I would practice my tricks in my room every single day and imagine what it would be like to be the next David Copperfield. It's all fun and games—until someone drops out of college.

If you ever want to see what crushing disappointment looks like, tell your ever-pragmatic, ex-physics-teacher, risk-averse father that you want to leave school to make a living with a childhood hobby that flouts the laws of science. It must have been hard for him to watch his youngest son throw away a chance at an education for a life of "Is this your card?"—the entertainment world's equivalent of, "Would you like fries with that?" It must have been even harder for him to watch me fail miserably.

Right out of high school, I quickly racked up over $16,000 in credit card debt (which in today's dollars is roughly $2.9 trillion. Well…it felt like that anyway). I had to get a side job at the mall to afford my car, gas, insurance, and rent payments. All the rent went straight to my dad. He had decided to start charging me $800 a month; it was tough love, an attempt at a reality intervention.

My magic career wasn't taking off. I couldn't understand it. By then I was getting pretty good. I mean, I wasn't teleporting or anything, but I could do some crazy stuff with elastics. I performed at a few little kids' birthday parties and one of the moms said I was swell.

Why hadn't I been discovered by a super-famous talent agent? Where were all the television producers? Why wasn't the world beating a path to my door?

Then a mentor of mine gave it to me straight. He said, "*Show business* is two words and *business* is the bigger one. You got the show, you need the business. Become a student of business. Become a student of sales and marketing. Study the science of influence."

"Influence?" I shuddered at the very word. "No thanks. If I'm going to trick people, I want it to be with their permission and for entertainment purposes only. I'm not interested in becoming some kind of used car magic pimp. Integrity is important to me."

"Okay, look at David Blaine. He doesn't do anything that other magicians can't do. He's only famous because of his business savvy."

"Flippin' David Blaine," I muttered. (When Blaine hit it big, he was the butt of a lot of jokes in the magic community. Sorry, David. We were just jealous.)

"Bad example then. Think of someone else instead. Think of someone you admire for their integrity."

"Okay, someone like Martin Luther King, Jr. or Abraham Lincoln comes to mind right away."

"Puh-leeze," he said. "Those are two of the most influential people in history. I thought you wanted to avoid influence because of your 'integrity'".

"Fair enough. Definitely my grandmother then. She never tried to influence anybody. She just quietly went about her life with humility, grace, and honor. She always put other people first and never had anything but a smile and a warm cup of tea."

"Hmm . . . Sounds like this grandmother of yours was a pretty big influence on you."

Check and mate.

For about a week, I remember feeling sick to my stomach at the idea of becoming a salesperson. I felt like Dr. McCoy from Star Trek. "Dammit Jim, I'm a magician, not a business person!"

Maybe you can relate. Maybe you've got a skill, a talent, a product, or an idea that you can't wait to share with the world—so long as you don't have to be the one to talk about it. Maybe it's because you think you're bad at selling, or maybe it's because you think selling is inherently bad. After all, many people associate sales with words like "manipulation," "persuasion," "coercion," or even "sleazy" or "creepy".

If that's you, then you're in the right book.

I have good news. My mentor didn't stop with the bad news. He didn't just say, "Influence is a necessary evil. You just have to deal with it." Sure, it's necessary, but it isn't necessarily evil. We may not have a choice in whether we influence others, but we do have a choice in *how* we influence them.

For me, that was the beginning of when influence got flipped.

WHAT HAPPENED NEXT

My mentor taught me the ins and outs of influence technique. Me. A die-hard, card-carrying, soft-spoken, easy-going, passive-to-a-fault *introvert*. Because of my personality, I thought I could never be influential. But I was wrong.

Once I realized that influence doesn't require fast-talking, schmoozing, or an awkward personality transplant, everything changed. I learned how to communicate authentically yet persuasively. I discovered influence strategies that even mild-mannered me could get excited about.

The very next month I performed twice as many magic shows as I had in the previous year. The month after that, I doubled it again. For the next eight years I was living my dream, averaging more than three hundred shows a year all around the United States. I didn't get better at magic; I got better at influence. I quit my day job, paid off all my debt, and moved out of my dad's house. He was so proud of me, he handed me an envelope containing all the rent money I had ever paid to him—a plan he'd had all along. It was quite the "dad of the year" moment. I'm probably going to steal that idea and use it when my own kids are old enough.

I mean, I'm not sure I'll give the money BACK, but charging rent…that's genius.

Some other magicians noticed my dramatic turnaround and wanted to know the secret to success. When I started helping them, I noticed a pattern. Those who couldn't get past their own mental roadblocks about influence couldn't succeed on even the lowest rung on the ladder of magical success—children's birthday parties.

Don't get me wrong, I've done my fair share of birthday parties. I remember once doing forty-eight in a single month. (This had the nice side effect of being a 99.8% effective birth control method. Trust me, you simply won't want kids after forty-eight birthday parties in thirty days.) You can make a living that way, but these parties aren't exactly considered the Rolls Royce of magic gigs.

The point is this: what magicians believed about influence seemed to determine if they were any good at it.

That's why I made sure to tell them the flower story.

Grab a seat, you'll want to hear this too…

THE FLOWER STORY

The summer was young and my wife had just earned her Master's degree in elementary education. Her father and I carpooled up to the campus for her graduation ceremony.

We were early and we had some time to kill. Directly in front of the main entrance were teddy bears and bouquets of flowers lined up neatly on the ground for sale. No storefront, just a display laid out on the sidewalk. The man running the show (the *floor*ist?) was pointing at merchandise and yelling out prices.

"Five for these! Ten for this! Twenty-five for a dozen!"

He had attracted quite a crowd. He was grabbing the money being waved at him like a game show contestant in a box.

Perhaps it was because I was so proud of my wife's hard work, dedication, and academic accomplishment. Or perhaps it was because even after five years of marriage, I was still trying to impress her dad. Either way, I grabbed a dozen roses from the most expensive side and handed the guy a couple of crumply bills.

They weren't the prettiest roses I had ever seen, but feeling satisfied that I had completed my husbandly duties, I looked over at Dad-in-Law.

"Let's grab some lunch," he said. "I don't wanna hafta carry a bunch of those around."

After enjoying a nearby sandwich shop special, we started walking the two blocks back to the main entrance. Directly across the street from the floral pitchman was another man, also selling flowers. However, there was no fancy display, no shouting, and certainly no money-shoving mob. Just a guy standing next to a cooler quietly asking passers-by, "Flowers? Anybody need flowers?" He looked more like a panhandler or an undercover agent than a street vendor. My father-in-law smelled an opportunity.

I have always had a great relationship with my father-in-law. The day I asked for his daughter's hand, he didn't hesitate. "Welcome to the family," he said with an embrace. But now that I have girls of my own, I understand why a natural, friendly, unspoken rivalry between the groom and the father of the bride is quite common.

My favorite example was the day my oldest daughter was born. He held her in his arms, looked into her sleepy eyes, and said loudly enough for everyone to hear, "Always remember…when Daddy says 'no,' Pépère says 'yes!'"

Point for Pépère.

"What do you got?" my father-in-law asked the mild-mannered flower vendor.

The vendor opened his cooler and took out some of his offerings. Compared to my dozen roses wrapped in plastic and held in place with a rubber band, his artful arrangements—complete with ribbon, baby's breath, and symmetry—were far superior.

"How much?"

"Ten for six and twenty for the dozen."

I couldn't believe it. "What?! That guy over there is selling these for twenty-five!"

"Hold on," the vendor said. "Let me see those."

What happened next might be a perfect example of why influence is so important. He took my roses, combined them with three of his, added the aforementioned accoutrements, and turned my flower frog into a prince—free of charge.

That's when I got really pissed.

This guy had a better product, better service, AND a better price. Yet I was forced to settle for second best because he failed to influence me to cross the street? He let the louder guy win—the guy shouting prices in his car lot radio commercial voice. Unacceptable.

Nice flower guy, if you're out there…this book is for you.

THE REST OF THIS BOOK

I'm glad you're here. Really. The fact that you're still reading tells me that you're a nice flower vendor.

Sure, you might not be selling flowers. Maybe you're someone trying to start a business and thinking that being "good" is good enough. Or maybe you're a new manager who earned your position because of your productivity, and you're realizing that your task-focused nature doesn't translate well to the people-focused job of management. Or maybe you're a salesperson with a conscience who needs to sell in order make ends meet, but you don't want to sell your soul in the process.

Or maybe you're just the kind of person who likes to skip book introductions.

Even if you did, there's no way you skipped the title of this book. It's huge. You can't miss it. You're in this book right now because influence is important to you. You're here because you've got a willingness, even an eagerness to learn. This isn't your first rodeo. Maybe you've tried building influence in the past, but results haven't been perfect.

You're not alone.

Moving someone from their point of view to yours is no small feat. The human brain is the most complex object in the known universe. Influence is complicated and difficult because people are complicated and difficult—more on this later.

Even if you do manage to influence someone's decision, there's no guarantee that their decision will result in any action. Has someone ever said to you, "Yes, I'll be there" or "I'll definitely get back to you" and then did not follow through? They weren't lying. It's just that as soon as you left, their old ways crept back. Maybe it didn't happen right away. Maybe it took a day, a week, or a month. The point is, influence that results in *lasting* action is the biggest challenge in all of human communication.

Have you ever tried to change someone else's mind or change their habits? Nearly impossible, right?

This is exactly why our understanding of the nature of influence needs to be flipped.

First, let's talk about what influence is not.

- Influence is NOT about getting other people to do things they don't want to do.

- Influence is NOT about using manipulative techniques to trick people into taking an action.

- Influence is NOT about being pushy, spammy, or salesy.

- Influence is NOT about pulling rank.

- Influence is NOT about issuing threats or punishments until people comply.

- Influence is NOT about sneaky brainwashing or mind control tricks.

Instead, influence is what parents do to help their kids to eat their vegetables. Sure, the kids may not want to at first. But it's the parent's job to not only provide the nutrition required for them to live and grow, but also to instill healthy eating habits that their children will take with them for the rest of their lives.

Influence is what doctors do to help their patients adopt the treatment plan or exercise plan that has been identified as the cure.

Influence is what consultative salespeople do to help their prospects save time or money by investing in the right product or service.

Influence is what leaders do to help their employees love their work and be fully engaged instead of feeling checked out or burnt out.

Influence is what managers do to motivate their team to help achieve the positive objectives of the organization.

Have you noticed a pattern? **"Influence is what people do to help."** If you're not helping others, then you're not doing it right. Specifically, influence is about helping people to overcome their short-term fears or discomforts so they can enjoy long term benefits. It isn't just about changing minds, it's about changing behaviors, habits, and even lives—and it's about changing them for the better.

Personally, I'm deeply grateful for those who have influenced and continue to influence me in my life. Mentors, friends, family, and sometimes even perfect strangers have all given me words of encouragement, friendly reminders, gracious examples, or sometimes even the slap in the face or kick in the butt that I needed to be my best self.

Influence is a worthy and noble pursuit. If nice-guy flower vendors don't figure this stuff out, then the loud rip-off artists will continue to draw the biggest crowds.

THAT'S WHY I'M HERE…
TO GIVE YOU THE SECRET SAUCE.

Until the early twentieth century, scientists had no idea about the existence of dark matter. No one did. It's always been there, but nobody talked about it. Everybody spent all their time, energy, and resources studying normal matter. For millennia, the world's brightest minds were focused on just the four percent of the universe that is normal, observable matter. The discovery of dark matter (and dark energy) opened the door to the other ninety-six percent. Breakthroughs came fast and furious and age-old mysteries were solved.

I believe the influence universe is primed for a similar breakthrough discovery. You probably picked up this book looking for more ways to flip people from their viewpoint to yours. You'll certainly get some of that. My real goal, however, is to flip your perspective of the true nature of influence. When you see what influence really is, then the entire game will change for you. Are you ready for the central theme of this book?

Influence is not only something you do, it's also something you have.

It's not just the observable stuff; your tactics, strategies, and techniques. It's also the hidden stuff; your relationships, your understanding of psychology, and your ethics. In fact, the vast majority of the influence game happens in the places that no one else seems to be noticing.

After over a decade of study, research, teaching, and practicing, I've consistently observed something that I call the T.R.U.E. Hierarchy of Influence. Think of this as a unified theory of influence—a complete picture of the influence universe including both the seen and the unseen. It's not one thing. Instead, it's four things arranged in a hierarchy. A hierarchy consists of levels, with each new level trumping the previous. The US military has its ranking system. If your rank is higher than someone else's rank, you win. No influence required, just a direct order. Corporations often operate with a similar hierarchical structure. If you're higher up the organization's chart than the next person, what you say carries more weight.

Hierarchies are useful in this way. They tell us who has the final word. They tell us where the power lies. Each level of the T.R.U.E. Hierarchy of Influence allows the communicator to carry more sway and create more influence. In some situations, and with some people, you may only need to operate at level one. Other situations will require a deeper level of influence. The higher levels will garner better long-term results, but you can't forgo the lower levels either. Each level builds upon the previous. Only the first level is what you do. The rest are about what you have.

LEVEL ONE: TECHNIQUE

Did you know that saying "Thanks in advance," at the end of an email will get you a 65.7% response rate, but closing with "Best," will only get you a 51.2% response rate? Did you know studies show that a citrus smell puts people in a more generous mood, and it also makes people more likely to put an offer on a house? Did you know that putting the most expensive option at the top of an order form increases the likelihood that it will be chosen? (The likelihood goes higher if it is one of three choices—not two and not four. It also helps if it is the exact same price as the not-as-good second option and it is printed on a sheet of goldenrod paper that the prospect has already written on.) There is certainly no shortage of techniques out there.

When people ask me how to become more influential, technique is what they often *think* they want. Whenever I do media appearances, the hosts eat up the techniques. My blog posts that feature "ninja mind control hacks" seem to get the most views, likes, and shares. During my keynote presentations, people perk right up and take furious notes whenever I describe a powerful psychological technique they've never heard of. Techniques are the *fun* part. You can use them the minute you learn them. When they work, you feel a sense of instant gratification. It feels like you've got mind control powers.

But when you're all out of techniques, you feel desperate. Every week I get an email or a comment on my blog asking, "What do I *say* to this person?" Sometimes there is a simple answer: a rewording of an email or a minor adjustment to one's approach that can make all the difference. But sometimes these people don't need more techniques. Sometimes they need to graduate to the next level.

LEVEL TWO: RELATIONSHIP

My late friend, magician and marketing consultant Eric Paul, used to say, "All things being equal, people do business with who they know, like, and trust." That's good advice, but not very provocative. Fortunately, he didn't stop there. After a meaningful pause, he'd continue with the real insight, "All things NOT being equal…people do business with who they know, like, and trust."

In other words, Mom is gonna buy candy bars from you even if she can get a better deal at Wal-Mart. There's nothing more powerful than a strong positive relationship. While you obviously can't be everyone's close relative, there are ways to quickly build rapport and maintain a solid connection built on trust. The flip-side is that when relationships break down, so does influence.

Higher-level, long-term strategies like authenticity, vulnerability, gratitude, patience, humility, graciousness, honesty, empathy, and others all help to build and solidify healthy relationships. It feels a bit strange to use a word like "strategies" to describe these traits, and I'll never suggest they should be used only as a means to an end. However, being an honest, genuine, caring person doesn't come naturally for everyone. For these people, the "strategy" should be to increase those relationship-boosting traits.

LEVEL THREE: UNDERSTANDING

You can drive a car without understanding how a carburetor works. Similarly, you can learn and use influence techniques without understanding the psychological nuts and bolts of how they work. So, Level One is perfectly attainable without understanding.

It is also common to reach Level Two without a clear understanding of why you just seem to "hit it off" with particular people. That's all well and fine for most people, most of the time. However, if you want to achieve real and lasting influence, understanding will be a requirement.

In this section, you'll hear why highly-advanced influencers (including an FBI hostage negotiator) value understanding so much and the painful lengths they'll go to just so they can increase it. For them, understanding literally is the difference between life and death.

My site, **MoreInfluential.com**, is dedicated to helping people develop a deeper understanding of others in a practical way. Have a visit. While you're there, sign up for email tips and tune-ups for keeping your influence game strong.

LEVEL FOUR: ETHICS

Do ethics really have a place in a book about influence? Is this just an obligatory disclaimer before we get to the section on Jedi mind tricks? Just about everyone will pay lip service to "ethical persuasion" because of moral considerations, but I want to ask more practical questions: Do strong ethics make you more influential?

When you draw an ethical line in the sand, are you shooting yourself in the foot? Are you giving everyone else permission to walk all over you? Do nice guys really finish last? Can you live and work among wolves without being forced to join the pack?

Look, I get it. It's a jungle out there. It's survival of the fittest. But perhaps maintaining a moral compass makes you a more fit influencer, not less.

Those who don't understand this hierarchy run into trouble when they try to become more influential. They might be very good at technique, but if their situation requires influence at the relationship level, they'll be disappointed with their results.

For example, Harold, a newly minted salesperson, decides to gain a competitive advantage by brushing up on his selling technique. He runs out and buys a stack of books on the topics of persuasion, neuro-linguistic programming, and hypnotic language patterns. He attends "Always Be Closing" sales seminars and learns all kinds of techniques for changing a no into a yes. He has a tool belt loaded with tried-and-true tricks like the confident handshake, the assumptive close, playing hard ball, low balling, phony rapport-building clichés, pacing statements, and there is no objection he can't overcome.

Like Liam Neeson's character in *Taken*, he's mastered a set of very specific skills. He systematically unleashes them onto his prospects, transforming features into benefits, tapping into their pain points, and pushing emotional hot buttons. Lo and behold, he gets the sale. Then another, and another.

He is killing his quota, consistently earning healthy commissions, rising up the leaderboard, and getting noticed by his superiors. He earns a promotion in no time flat and becomes a sales manager. Things seem to be going well for Harold.

That's when the wheels start to fall off the bus.

Now that he has a sales team, he attempts to use the same manipulation tactics on them that have served him so well on the sales floor. The only problem is, those tactics come from the wrong level. Level One is fine for one-time transactions, but not for longer-term relationships with employees. Without graduating to the higher levels, Harold's trustworthiness erodes and his relationships suffer. The team turns on him. Their productivity goes down as their performance drops to a bare minimum, all the while grumbling behind Harold's back.

At the same time, if Harold decided to forget all his technique and focus exclusively on being *liked* by his employees, he would run the risk of losing their respect. His authority would suffer. The levels build upon one another.

In the next section, we'll look at several true stories of real people creating real influence and getting real results. I'll organize them using the T.R.U.E. Hierarchy of Influence. You'll learn how techniques were used to build a school, remove the splinter of the century, get someone to actually respond to an email, overcome an imaginary disease, and much more.

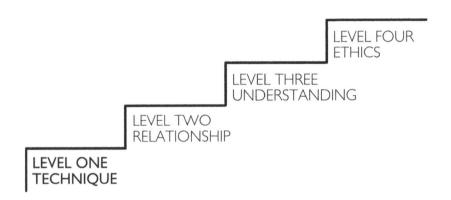

LEVEL FOUR
ETHICS

LEVEL THREE
UNDERSTANDING

LEVEL TWO
RELATIONSHIP

LEVEL ONE
TECHNIQUE

The nineteenth-century preacher, Henry Melvill wrote: "A thousand fibers connect us with our fellow men; and along these fibers, as sympathetic threads, our actions run as causes, and they come back to us as effects."

There are two ideas that I want you to take from Melvill's quote. First, if you want to change the effect, then you must change the cause. All of the techniques in Level One are various attempts at changing the outcome of a situation (the effect) by altering your words and actions (the cause). It's tempting to think that we have no control over other people's actions, but we do play a role. This fact should offer hope—not blame—to any reader who has ever been frustrated by their interactions with other humans.

Second, it's complicated. *A thousand fibers?* That's a lot of moving parts. Just because there's a cause-and-effect relationship, that doesn't mean it's always easy to see what that relationship is. Sometimes an important technique might appear unrelated or unimportant to your ultimate influence goal. For example, a traveling salesperson once told me that he gets his best results when he wears a black shirt and a black sport coat during his presentations. It seems strange that the color of his clothing could impact the outcome of someone else's decision to buy. But when it comes to influence techniques, there are a thousand fibers. Everything makes a difference.

THE SCHOOL THAT WORDS BUILT

A few years back, I invited my blog readers to submit their biggest influence problem. I asked, "Who do you need to influence and why?" Most of the responses were from people who wanted to sell more product, get their employees to listen, get their kids to behave, or get their employees to stop behaving like kids who don't behave. But this was one of my favorite responses:

> "I am the Chair of the School Building Committee in my town and we are trying to persuade the community to support a major school construction project. We have not constructed a new school, nor completed any major renovations in more than fifty years. I must instill a sense of need in the community at large so that we can ensure a new school is constructed for the children."

This is exactly why I'm so passionate about influential communication. Here's a guy who wanted a new school for his kids, but over fifty years of inertia stood in his way. In order to build this school, he had to build his case. As always, to move mountains we must be able to move people.

I responded with some ideas and suggestions. Two years later, he sent me a follow up email with a link to an online video of the town meeting. I watched his TED talk-length presentation while proudly noting the influence strategies he used. Then came the big moment. The moderator invited anyone who wanted to approve the new school to please rise. Out of the 981 people present, 961 of them stood up in unison.

His email further detailed the victory.

> *"There was also a larger ballot vote and again the school was approved. This time by 83% of the voters. Construction has begun and is on pace to be completed on time. Thanks for your guidance... it made a world of difference in the way I approached the situation."*

Don't you love a happy ending?

The $96.4M school that words built

The rest of this chapter is an updated and expanded version of the email I sent him. It will outline the advice and scripts I suggested and explain the strategies the committee chair used to get this $96.4M project approved.

DON'T BE IMPOTENT

Have you ever noticed that most people seem to be completely unmoved by things like logic and facts? Has telling someone "Smoking is bad for you" EVER worked? When attempting to influence, don't use arguments aimed at the reasonable, logical prefrontal cortex. Instead, make sure your approach taps into the far more powerful emotional circuitry of the brain.

This means changing, "It's been fifty years since we've built a school" to "How long are we prepared to wait before our children get the educational facilities they deserve?" This means that saying "Kids' test scores have steadily declined by X% each year because of deteriorating building conditions" becomes "Meet Jonny. He's in first grade and he loves baseball. Last week he was sitting in class and he nearly had a heat stroke because there's no air-conditioning in the building. There are hundreds of kids like Jonny and they need your help."

Another simple, yet powerful way to engage emotion is by tapping into what psychologists call "anticipation of regret." You might say something like "We're at a crossroads. I'm concerned that we're making the wrong decision not to build. I fear that in a year, *we'll look back on today with great regret* if we vote not to give our kids the facilities they need."

STORYTIME

Stories will always be among our most powerful communication tools. Our brains are wired to tune in to every "Once upon a time," and every "Meet Jonny".

Is there another town that recently built a school? Did it have a wonderful effect on the entire community? If so, use the "Then, Now, How" formula. It works like this:

1. The other town was just like us. Same situation. Same problems. (THEN)

2. They are now enjoying amazing results with fewer problems. (NOW)

3. They did all of this by building a new school. (HOW)

EVERYONE ELSE IS DOING IT

As it turns out, there *was* another town that had recently built a school. A bunch of them, in fact. Out of the thirty-seven towns in the area, thirty-six of them had built a new school or had completed major renovations in the previous few years.

The follow-the-crowd mentality runs deep within our brain's circuitry. If a mob of people is running past you in the same direction, it's completely natural to assume that you should probably start running too. Whether or not we like to admit it, we are heavily influenced by crowds. The people at the town meeting couldn't help but wonder, "If literally every other town and city in the area is doing it, why not us?"

SEE?

Humans are primarily visual beings. Almost a third of our brains is dedicated to visual processing. My favorite piece of evidence for our visual preference is known as the McGurk Effect, an interesting illusion that occurs when you dub a certain kind of audio over a certain kind of video. For example, I did a web search for "McGurk Effect," and right now I'm looking at a video of someone speaking a syllable repetitively. I can clearly see his mouth forming the sound, "ba." At one point, he switched and now he's saying "fa." Only he never really said "fa" at all. Even though I would have sworn up and down that he said "fa," it was just an illusion.

The narrator explained what happened. Only the image changed. While his lips were forming the syllable "fa," the audio remained the same. However, my brain prioritized the visual input I received over the audio input. So even though my computer's speakers were clearly pumping out "ba" audio, my brain still perceived it as "fa" because of the McGurk effect. In a direct battle between auditory and visual stimuli, visual wins every time.

During his presentation, our hero showed a map of thirty-six surrounding towns, each color-coded by how recently a new school was built or a major school renovation completed. His town was the ONLY one whose color stood in stark contrast to the rest. It was like a gaping black hole in a sea of bright stars. While his town hadn't seen school construction or renovation in over fifty years, all of the rest had school construction projects completed within the previous two. I felt like I was looking at the most obvious game of "Which one of these is not like the other?" in the history of ever.

The color-coded map was a compelling visual aid that made the committee chair's message much more memorable and persuasive.

NOW BUYERS AND LATER PAYERS

The major downside to building a new school is that it ain't cheap. It cost $96.4 million, to be exact. Ouch.

When watching the presentation, I picked up on a key phrase that helped voters get past that. He said, "Taxes won't start going up until two years from now."

"Two years from now?" says your brain. "That might as well be never!" Our brains have a hard time identifying with our future selves. That's why credit card companies offer us twelve months interest-free (and then slap us with back interest if we don't pay off every cent before the clock runs out.) "Buy now, pay later" will always be appealing.

FREE/NOW

For whatever reason, certain words are just more influential than others.[1] Our hero wisely began his entire presentation by alluding to one of the best.

> *"We have been offered a distinct opportunity to utilize grant funding that will pay for more than half the construction costs."*

"Grant" is a word that means *free*. Free is good. We like free. We'll take something that's free even if we don't really need it, just because it was free. In fact, "free" is such a compelling word that it's probably better to state it outright rather than implying it or using a synonym. In fact, if I had to do a quick re-write of that opening line, I would recommend saying it this way...

---

1. www.MagicWordsBook.com

"Right now, we are being offered a distinct opportunity to utilize free grant funding that will pay for more than half of the construction."

Here's what I changed and why:

- Nothing fancy with the word "free." I just crammed in there and let it work its magic.

- I removed the word "costs." We don't like things that cost.

- I added "now" to create a sense of urgency. "Now" implies "but maybe not later." Dr. Robert Cialdini, in his seminal work, *Influence: The Psychology of Persuasion*, explains why "now" is such a powerful motivator:

"As opportunities become less available, we lose freedoms; and we hate to lose the freedoms we already have. This desire to preserve our established prerogatives is the centerpiece of psychological reactance theory, developed by psychologist Jack Brehm to explain the human response to diminishing personal control. According to the theory, whenever free choice is limited or threatened, the need to retain our freedoms makes us desire them significantly more than previously."

ABSOLUTELY/GUARANTEED

After the presentation, residents were invited to ask questions. A lady stood up and expressed a concern about water runoff from the school's fields possibly affecting nearby homes. She asked, "Can you guarantee that this won't be a problem?"

My heart dropped and I held my breath. "Uh-oh," I thought.

Then he gave the best possible response. *"We absolutely can."*

Bang. Complete confidence. He spoke with unquestionable authority. In addition to that, he invited an expert to the microphone to explain exactly WHY they were so confident that building the new school not only wouldn't make the runoff worse, but it would actually IMPROVE the area's drainage system.

People are risk-averse. They aren't comfortable even if there's only a one percent chance of something going wrong. Guarantee that there is NO risk and communicate that guarantee with authority, and people will follow your lead.

And the town residents did follow his lead! Obviously no communication is perfect, but in this case, the results speak for themselves. This was a very persuasive presentation. At the end of the day, the right decision was made. I hope this brief case study helps even more people to do even more good by respectfully using the power of influential communication outlined here and in the rest of this volume.

THE SPLINTER OF THE CENTURY

My daughter Sophie and I were basking in the sun on our pressure-treated deck, barefoot, when it happened. She wasn't running, jumping, or even plodding along like a happy toddler. She was holding my hand and standing virtually still. There were no tears either, just a small, "Ow!"

I brought her inside and took a look. There was a small cut at the base of her big toe. It looked like she might have a splinter, so I grabbed the tweezers and tried to pull it out. She jumped a mile every time I touched her foot. I thought she was exaggerating. Then I saw it. The other end of the splinter was visible through the skin of her foot. It was more than three inches long; I thought it was a nail. That's when I brought her to the ER.

The doctors there couldn't remove it. They gave me two options. "Neither of them good," they said:

1. Surgery with anesthesia.

2. Leave it in and "maybe it will work itself out" while antibiotics fight the impending infection.

After discussing it with my wife, surgery seemed the obvious choice. This baby wasn't going to work itself out.

Here's where it gets interesting.

I was told in the ER, "Okay, there is a surgeon on call. He will be in to take a look at it."

After waiting almost an hour, no surgeon came. Instead, they passed along a message. "He said to call first thing Monday morning and make an appointment for Tuesday."

"Great!" I thought. "Surgery on Tuesday and we'll get this thing taken care of!"

That's not at all what happened. When I called on Monday, I was told, "Nope. Can't make an appointment for surgery if the surgeon hasn't even seen the patient yet. Make an appointment for Tuesday. At that point, we can schedule her surgery for later in the week IF NECESSARY. Besides, the ER report says that the foreign object was already removed."

WHAT?!

If I followed their directions my daughter would have had to leave a chunk of pressure-treated wood inside her foot for as many as six days. No school, no swimming, days out of work for Mommy and Daddy, and don't forget the pain! This was clearly not acceptable.

After several phone calls to multiple hospitals, I was told in no uncertain terms, "You can't just bring someone in for surgery. They MUST be seen and an appointment MUST be scheduled. Our surgeons simply can't fit you in until the end of the week. It's impossible."

Influence technique to the rescue! Here is some of the language I used...

> "Sandra (not her real name), I know this feels like it's impossible right now. But what if this was your kid?"

"Obviously, you and I both know that as her father, I can't leave this in her foot for one day, let alone as many as six."

"Look, we both want the same thing here and you come across as the type of person who knows how to get things done. I'm counting on you. I need your help."

"There is an absolute zero percent chance that the ER doctors removed the object. I'm looking at it right now and if you were here with me, all I'd have to do is point at it. Instead, you're going to have to trust me. Is it possible the ER report has a mistake?"

However, the *most important element* of what I did cannot be communicated through text on a page. What really took place on the phone was…

A RESPECTFUL TRANSFER OF EMOTION

This is an essential tactic for influence. The only reason the hospital workers weren't bending over backward to fit my daughter in was because they didn't feel the same urgency that I did. All they had was an ER report (that was riddled with multiple errors). I had a four-year-old with big, sad eyes. My job was to make them FEEL the way they needed to feel in order to be moved to action.

A HAPPY ENDING

It worked. After a long pause, the receptionist came back on the phone and asked, "Tim, has she had anything to eat today?"

"No, not since 8pm last night." That was true, which is a lesson in itself. I was *expecting a successful outcome,* so I kept her away from food so she'd be prepared for when they took her in.

I heard a slow sigh on the other end of the line, then, "Can you bring her in right now?"

"Yes! Thank you, I'll see you soon!"

We were in and out of surgery that morning and Sophie turned out just fine.

Most people transfer emotion by yelling, screaming, and cursing in order to get their way. That approach is not only exhausting, but it's not particularly effective either. Whenever you need to persuade or motivate someone, remember the lesson of Sophie's foot: *"Persuasion is a transfer of emotion."*

To see a photo of Sophie's splinter, visit:
www.MoreInfluential.com/sophiesfoot

THE VEGETABLE WAR

My kids used to hate fruits and vegetables. If there were vegetables on their plates, our dinner conversation felt less like family bonding time and more like a hostage negotiation. When they did take a bite, they might as well have been on *Fear Factor*, the show where contestants are forced to eat live worms, raw pig's tongue, or any number of unthinkables. The drama that a single slice of carrot could cause was remarkable. When the dust finally settled, my wife and I would look at all the nutrition left on their plates and wonder how the kids managed to survive on bread alone.

We tried several techniques...

BRIBERY

"If you take five big bites, then I'll give you a listening ticket." Listening tickets could be accumulated and exchanged for special privileges like screen time. They could also be taken away as punishment. Rewarding positive behavior is just as important, if not more important, than punishing unwanted behavior. However, using if/then bribes only works in the short term, if at all. My book *Magic Words* has a chapter on the word "if" and the dangers of using if/then bribes. If you're going to use rewards as motivators, then give the rewards as a surprise after the fact, not as a bribe dangled like a carrot—I mean, like a Twinkie.

NEXT FOOD IN

Any uneaten food would go back in the fridge and become tomorrow's breakfast. If they didn't eat it then, it was lunch. Eventually hunger took over and the plate would be clean. We told them, "These vegetables will be the next food you eat, no matter how long it takes you." Sure, we got some clean plates, but this only reinforced their bad associations with vegetables. The vegetables they were eating were cold and soggy. Not the best way to foster a lifelong love affair with healthy eating.

THE TROJAN HORSE

We'd hide the vegetables in dishes they enjoyed. "Is that good? Yeah? HA! You just ate an onion and LIKED IT!" Proving people wrong against their will is never a good idea. It backfires every time.

"HE'S WITH ME"

We'd smear celery with peanut butter. Broccoli was drenched in ranch dressing. The peanut butter and ranch dressing had backstage passes. Our children would easily let them past the exclusive velvet rope. "You're with peanut butter? Okay, come on in. Just don't cause any trouble."

This made them love peanut butter and ranch dressing even more. The vegetables were just glorified, edible utensils. Tolerated, but untasted.

LOGIC

"Do you like French Fries?"

"Yes."

"Well mashed potatoes are just the inside parts of French Fries."

"Well, I guess I only like the outside parts of French Fries then."

PEER PRESSURE

"Your friends eat their veggies. Don't you want to be like your friends?"

"Daddy, I thought you told me to follow my own path, be my own person, and make my own decisions no matter what other people do."

Outsmarted again.

ARTS AND CRAFTS

We'd use apples and raisins to make lady bugs and we'd turn strawberries and whipped cream into little Santa Clauses. This worked great and they ate every bite, but the novelty wore off quickly...for me. A forty-minute project to get them to eat a half of an apple and six raisins? There had to be a better way.

EXPOSURE THERAPY

They say it takes several exposures to a new idea or a new food before someone accepts

it. This is why companies pummel you with advertising messages. This is why the radio station plays that same song over and over until it "grows on you." Maybe we could get vegetables to grow on our kids by persistently exposing them?

My brother turned us on to Hello Fresh, a food delivery service similar to Blue Apron. Every week a large box would arrive on our doorstep, full of ice packs and fresh ingredients. There were three complete recipes in each shipment, and everything was pre-measured to the exact right portions. All we had to do was cook it.

Each recipe was healthy and delicious, and because we chose the vegetarian option, each box was full of fresh veggies. There were foods I never knew existed and combinations of foods that I never would have imagined myself. These veggies were putting their absolute best foot forward.

When we got our first delivery, we excitedly tore it open and had a look. It didn't take long for the kids to spot all the vegetables. Onions, carrots, mushrooms, spinach, kale, beets, etc. "Ewww! What is THAT?" they said as they pointed to the ginger root.

"Oooh, I LOVE the smell of ginger!" my wife said.

The novelty of discovery quickly wore off and one night my older, sassier daughter asked what we were having for dinner. I said, "Hello Fresh."

She made a face and said, "More like 'Goodbye Fresh.'" My brother's kids called it "Hello Yucky." I didn't get it. The recipes tasted like candy to me. Why were kids so resistant?

THE TURNAROUND

One day I put a cutting board in front of my oldest daughter. I handed her a sharp knife and some carrots from the minestrone soup recipe box.

"Wanna help me cook?"

She looked at the knife and looked at me with an expression of disbelief. "Can I?"

"Of course! The recipe says to peel and dice the carrots, so here's what we do..."

I got her started, and she was off to the races. Her little sister came down to see what was going on. She wanted to join the fun as well. I handed her a cutting board, a carrot, and a slightly less sharp knife.

They dove in to their task. Every cut was like a little mini-commitment to the soup.

Before I knew it, all the ingredients sat in little glass bowls just like on the cooking shows. Music was playing and we were tossing veggies, beans, and broth into a big pot over a medium flame. It was *FUN*.

Best of all, the kids *couldn't wait* to try the soup when it was finished.

"What do you think?"

"Daddy, it's sooooo gooood!" they said as they devoured every last bite, veggies and all. There was no way their brains would let them say "Hello Yucky" this time because it was *THEIR* soup.

Always remember: People support what they create.

HOW TO GENERATE SUDDEN INTEREST IN OLD IDEAS

Sudden interest.

It's the stuff of legend.

Van Gogh died a broke and lonely man. Now he's one of the most famous artists of all time. By the time he was 35, all of Herman Melville's books were out of print and he had only earned about $10,000 from writing in his entire lifetime. Moby Dick got its due acclaim about forty years later, after his death. Similarly, only a small handful of Emily Dickinson's poems were published during her lifetime. Many forward-thinking individuals do not live to see their ideas catch on.

Today, I want to give you a way to create sudden interest in your idea. Preferably BEFORE you die.

Almost three years after the release of *Magic Words*, there was a sudden, unexplained boost in sales. This is a graph of the weekly sales numbers taken from the publisher's web site:

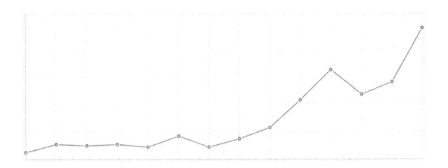

So, what's the deal? What caused the sudden interest?

It turns out that another book with "Magic Words" in its subtitle had been selling very well around the same time. Online retailers began offering my book as an add-on, and buyers were going for it.

There is a powerful lesson hidden in the psychology here. The customer is essentially saying, "Well, here's a book that is similar to another book I already want. Therefore, I must want this book too." That's the key for getting an idea to catch on. Make it similar to an idea they already accept.

Here's a quick story to illustrate how you can use this principle of similarity to move your ideas forward.

The Lion King is a classic Disney movie that almost didn't get made. The powers that be were having a hard time figuring out what to do with the script. They weren't sure if they even liked it. Finally, someone used the principle of similarity...

"It's like Hamlet, but with Lions."

Click.

Suddenly, everything made sense. Suddenly, the script fell into place. Suddenly, there was INTEREST in getting the film made sooner rather than later.

Use the following formula to generate sudden interest in your own ideas...

"It's like _____,
but/with/without/for/of _____"

A few examples…

Dave and Busters: It's like Chuck E Cheese for adults.

Sport Clips: They're like Hooters, but for haircuts.

Instagram: It's like Facebook, but with pictures.

Thunderclap: It's like Kickstarter, but for social sharing.

HOW TO ASK FOR SOMETHING IN AN EMAIL

Asking for help is hard enough without having to put it into email form. Text on a screen is completely devoid of those handy nonverbal elements. How can you ask for help effectively without sounding needy, entitled, or worse, getting ignored entirely? These tips should help.

WHAT'S WRONG WITH A PHONE CALL?

When asking for help, the first decision is whether or not email is even the right tool for the job. It's certainly easier to fire off an email and not have to deal with any possible rejection face-to-face, but does it give you the best chance of receiving the help? Email is perceived, and rightly so, as impersonal. Many people would agree that they are more likely to help if you pick up the phone and call them. If possible, maybe you even want to go and see them in person.

These options are not always practical though. Maybe you don't have the number, or the person you're trying to reach has a really good gatekeeper in place. Maybe they're just too busy or otherwise inaccessible. You can't always get someone on the phone or nose-to-nose, so email is the next logical choice. But how should you go about it?

FIND YOUR CONFIDENCE BALANCE

If someone thinks you're an ungrateful beggar, then they'll be very unlikely to offer you any help at all. However, stubbornly refusing to accept help is the other extreme and should also be avoided.

If you're timid about asking for help, then I have good news. It is perfectly okay to do so. In fact, people inherently WANT to help you.

Emma Seppälä writes in her blog[2] about how the desire to help others is intrinsic in humans:

> "Michael Tomasello and other scientists at the prestigious Max Planck Institute have found that even infants too young to have been conditioned by the conventions of politeness will automatically engage in helpful behavior. Research conducted by Dale Miller at the Stanford Business School shows that adults, too, are instinctively driven to help others."

However, people stop wanting to help when they feel any hint of ingratitude.

So, before you start writing, find your confidence balance. Feel good in knowing that people want to help, but don't become arrogant and expect it, or worse, demand it.

You'll know that you've got the right balance when you give up your right to be angry or hurt when they say no.

---

2. https://emmaseppala.com/service-it-does-you-so-good

DO YOUR RESEARCH

Don't blast out a stock email pitch blindly to a list of people you hope to receive help from. Individual emails to individual people will take longer than bulk email, but this approach has a much better chance for success. Find out who they are, find out how they prefer to be contacted, and find something that might be relevant to them right now. By looking at their web site or social media profiles for two minutes before you write your email, you'll stand out from the clutter of everyone else who didn't take the time to do so.

ALWAYS ADDRESS THEM BY NAME

Leading with "Dear Sir/Madam" or some other generic salutation is an immediately deletable offense. A person's name carries significant psychological weight. A simple "Hi Jim," is all it takes to tap into its attention-grabbing power. Dale Carnegie said, "A person's name is, to that person, the sweetest and most important sound in any language."

He had no idea just how right he was.

USE THE LETTERS IN THEIR NAME

Modern science has shown that the human brain not only over-focuses on the sound of one's own name, but it also gives extra attention to the letters in that name (particularly the first letter).[3]

A few examples:

- People whose names begin with T are more likely to purchase Toyotas than Hondas.

---

3. http://www.sicotests.com/psyarticle.asp?id=99

- People whose names begin with J are more likely to live in Jacksonville than Albuquerque.

- People whose names begin with C are more likely to prefer Coke to Pepsi.

- People whose names begin with K are more likely to marry Kim than Lori.

Want to grab someone's attention in an email? Use their name AND use more words that prominently feature the same letter as their name.

For example, tell Fran that your product is fabulous, fantastic, or affordable, and tell Gary that your company is great and going places. Tell Tom that it's a time-saver and tell Mike that it's a money-maker. Offer Dan a deal but offer Barbara a bargain.

START WITH THE PHRASE, "I NEED YOUR HELP."

Another word featured in my book *Magic Words* was "help." Like all magic words, "help" taps into a powerful psychological motivator. In this case, it's the same motivator that was discovered by Dale Miller's research mentioned above—people WANT to help.

"I need your help" flips a switch in their minds and lets them know you are giving them an opportunity to exercise that deep desire to help others. Unfortunately, that feeling of helpfulness is short-lived and can quickly morph back into resistance and self-interest. Let's look at how to avoid that.

DO NOT TRIGGER RESISTANCE

The word "not" can often become a resistance trigger. Phrases like, "This won't take up a whole lot of time," or "Don't feel any pressure to do this," are meant to alleviate resistance and increase the likelihood the person will help, but in actual fact, they can have the opposite effect. To see how this works, try to follow these instructions:

Do not think of the word "hippopotamus" for the next ten seconds.

How'd you do?

The apparent intention was to have you "not" think of hippopotamus, but the result was quite different. Most people report not being able to get the word "hippopotamus" out of their head!

In your emails, communicate what things are, not what they are not.

Other possible resistance phrases to be avoided are:

- "It will cost you nothing." (Replace with, "It's free.")

- "It'll only take five minutes of your time," (Replace with, "I'd like to spend five minutes with you.")

- "Don't hesitate to contact me." (Replace with, "Contact me at _____")

- "I know you're busy, but..." (Replace with, "I respect your time and...")

GET TO THE POINT

Assume that they are busier than you. Don't give a long-winded description of your problem in hopes that they will figure out what they should be doing to help you fix it. Ask them precisely and directly what they can do to help you.

THIS WORD IS *KILLING* YOUR CREDIBILITY

James Pennebaker studies how people use words. More specifically, how they use function words (such as pronouns and articles). His findings are startling and nearly universal. In his book *The Secret Life of Pronouns*, he writes, "In any interaction between two people, the person with the higher status uses fewer I-words. [They also] use first person plural pronouns (we, us, our) at much higher rates than those lower in status."

When emailing for help, your perceived status is important. People are more likely to help people who are similar to themselves. That's why a sentiment of, "You remind me of myself at your age," can often precede help. Remove as many I words as you can from your emails and replace them with "we" words and "you" words.

BE CAREFUL OF REWARDS

The moment you offer a promise or reward in exchange for help, you enter the world of transactions instead of relationships. The power of the word *help* wanes significantly when coupled with transactional thinking. The moment you offer a reward is the moment it ceases to become "help" at all.

WAIT A WEEK

If they don't respond to your first email, wait a week. Then, when you follow up with a simple, "Just following up to see if you got this," message, they'll feel guilty for not responding. This is much more likely to elicit a "yes" response than the annoyance they'll feel if you email them every day.

SAY THANKS BEFORE, DURING, AND AFTER

Nothing kills a helpful mood faster than ingratitude or entitlement on your part. You may think the word "thanks" has become meaningless or trite with overuse, but just try and remove it. A thankless interaction can burn a bridge for any future help you might receive. Type "Thanks in advance!" in your initial request, say thanks again when they accept, and say it again one more time when they deliver.

The email app Boomerang analyzed over 350,000 email threads and found that if you want to get a response, how you sign off matters a great deal:

CLOSING:	RESPONSE RATE:
thanks in advance	65.7%
thanks	63.0%
thank you	57.9%
cheers	54.4%
kind regards	53.9%
regards	53.5%
best regards	52.9%
best	51.2%
Baseline (all emails in sample)	47.5%

Looks like "Best" isn't the best after all. (Although it is better than average.)

So, if you want a response to your emails, signing off with "Thanks in advance" gives you the best chance.

There you have thirteen different ideas for making a personal request via email. Use as many as you can as often as you can, and your chances of getting a "yes" will go way up.

WRITING A PERSUASIVE SPEECH—THE ACA FORMULA

Being persuasive in an email is one thing. You've got plenty of time to edit and re-type. But public speaking is *hard*. It's live, it's real-time, and everyone is watching. How can we do it more effectively and more persuasively?

Here are my answers from a lifetime of blowing into microphones…

If you've got to give a presentation, then chances are you want to make it persuasive. If the audience doesn't behave or believe *differently* than they did before they heard you, then you simply didn't do your job as a speaker.

You've probably heard the classic public speaking formula a zillion times:

1. **Tell them what you're going to tell them.**

2. **Tell them.**

3. **Tell them what you've told them.**

That might be okay for informative speeches, but it's terrible for persuasive speeches. And it's boring. SOOOOO boring!

Telling is NOT selling. Being informative is simply not good enough to influence the human brain.

As a professional speaker, I use a fairly complex process to craft my talks (which includes a three-step framework and a 50 Point Public Speaking Checklist that I'll never deliver a speech without.)

Whether it's a twenty-minute "lunch and learn" webinar, a sixty-minute keynote address, or a full-day management training, the basic formula remains the same.

You can download my 50 Point Checklist for free at www.MoreInfluential.com/business. For my three-step framework…just keep reading.

PUBLIC SPEAKING TIP: A MAZE IS MUCH EASIER TO SOLVE *BACKWARDS*.

Influencing someone is a complex, daunting task. The process of going from where they are to where you want them to be can often seem maze-like.

I have a secret: Do it backwards.

What do you want them to do after hearing your speech? Decide that FIRST.

For example, let's say you want to convince non-voters to get out and vote. That's the end of your maze. Now we can work our way backward from there.

You can't just say, "Go vote." That won't carry any weight. You've got to build a *connection* with them first.

Therefore, the step before "call to action" is to "build connection."

But wait…how can you build a connection if no one is listening to you? Before we build connection we must first earn their *attention*.

And that's my *Three-Step Public Speaking Framework*: Attention, Connection, Action (ACA).

Follow these guidelines and you'll be well on your way to a great speech!

STEP ONE: ATTENTION

GOAL: Make them think, "This will be different, I like this person, and this will be fun."

You've only got a few moments, so think hard about what you can do to accomplish the important goals above.

Consider:

- Expressing similarity ("I remember sitting right where you are now…")
- Using humor (especially self-deprecating)
- Communicating novelty ("This will be unlike anything you've ever heard before on the topic of influence")
- Dressing distinctly
- Walking in from the back of the room instead of from the wings

Body language is the fastest and best way to grab attention. Here's a crash course on good body language: **www.udemy.com/body-language**

STEP TWO: CONNECTION

GOAL: Make them think, "This relates to my life, and it is simple enough for me to do."

If it's not relevant to my life, you've lost me. If it's too complicated, you've lost me. I can't fix global warming, but I can cast a vote. Connect your message to me (especially through storytelling), and you've got a chance.

Consider:

- **Stating their problem or their possibility.** A problem is about pain; possibility is about gain. (Keep in mind, the desire to avoid pain is twice as powerful as the desire to gain pleasure.)

  Examples:

  - "How many of you are tired of negative people and chronic complainers in the workplace?" (Problem)

  - "I've uncovered a little-known niche that can bring you more customers than you can imagine." (Possibility)

- **Simplifying your message.** Just because you are an expert on your topic doesn't mean your audience wants to become experts too. A confused mind does NOTHING. There's no faster way to make an audience tune you out than to overload them with information.

- **Sharing a "mess to success" story - featuring you as the "guide."**

  Example:

  - "Toni was failing as a manager. Her team wasn't

performing, yet she was the one taking all the blame. She wanted to be the 'cool boss' so she tried being everyone's friend. That backfired. Then she tried 'laying down the law'. That backfired too! It all changed when she discovered the power of my influential communication framework. Suddenly, her team genuinely respects her, they are more productive and creative than ever before, and her boss gave her a raise!"

Toni is the hero. She's the one everyone can relate to. If she can do it, they can do it. You're merely the guide who helped make it all possible. Donald Miller of StoryBrand teaches that too many people try to be the hero. Instead, he suggests taking on the role of Yoda so the audience can feel like Luke Skywalker.

STEP THREE: ACTION

GOAL: Encourage them to ACT!

Too often, we either forget to ask, or we're afraid to ask. Don't forget a direct call-to-action in your speech. Tell them exactly what you want them to do. Don't be shy and don't make them guess. Spell it out.

Consider:

- **Sharing a closing story.**

  This last story should convey how you want the audience to feel when they leave. If you want them to feel energized, tell an energetic story. There is almost nothing more captivating or more persuasive than a good story.

- **Delivering one last one-liner that tells them exactly what you want them to do next.**

- *Example:* "Remember…Grab your coat and go out to VOTE!" (Bonus points if it rhymes.)

SPEAKING OF BONUS…

Don't forget to download my free *50 Point Public Speaking Tips Checklist*. This handy guide will tell you exactly what you need to add to (or take away from) your speech. You'll never miss an important point or forget to do something obvious during your presentation again.

GET THE PUBLIC SPEAKING CHECKLIST HERE:
http://www.moreinfluential.com/business

What about those persuasive speeches that are delivered to just one person? In business this is called an "elevator pitch." David Newman, author of *Do It! Marketing* calls this a "verbal business card." Let's have a look at that in the next chapter.

THE ELEVATOR PITCH FOR YOUR ELEVATOR PITCH

Ah, the elevator pitch. A favorite tool of the networking masses. A rite of passage of sorts. You've heard the scenario: you step into an elevator and go up one floor. The elevator doors open, and in walks the client of your dreams. They start some small talk and ask, "What do you do?" You've got the rest of the elevator ride to respond. How do you answer that in twenty seconds in such a way that gets them interested? The answer is simple.

You don't.

When people ask, "What do you do?" they're just making conversation to be nice. They don't really care. Their polite attention will only last about twenty seconds. That's why you've been taught to keep your elevator pitch short. But frankly, that's stupid. Even the best elevator pitches have a very low success rate, no matter how short they are.

Instead, the best use of that initial grace period is to make a bid for an attention extension. If you can pique their interest, they'll hold the elevator door and listen to you all day long. That's why you need an elevator pitch for your elevator pitch.

Mine has four parts. It all starts when someone asks me that all-too-common question:

"What do you do?"

"You mean, in addition to the obvious? Being an international bodybuilding champion?" (I'm 5'11" and a buck thirty, soaking wet. When I step on ants, they live. It's painfully clear that I'm not an international bodybuilding champion.)

They'll either laugh, or they'll look at me with a confused expression. Either way, it's exactly the effect I want (for reasons I will explain later). Then I continue…

"Well, you know how email, texting, and social media have pretty much taken over how we communicate?"

"Yes."

"We're more connected than ever, but yet…more disconnected than ever. So, I teach managers the secrets of creating true connections in their teams in a way that gets immediate results."

"How do you do that?" (or "What do you mean?" or "What kind of results?")

Boom. Done. That's my entire elevator pitch for my elevator pitch.

I've quickly earned far more than twenty seconds of their attention by turning a pitch into a conversation. Let's unpack the four steps:

1. START WITH A VERBAL SLAP.

If someone isn't paying full attention to you, I give you permission to slap them (Verbally, of course.)

A verbal slap is the first order of business for a good elevator pitch's elevator pitch. You've got to contradict their expectations. When someone asks, "What do you do?" they're engaged in a pattern of social behavior that they've coasted through a thousand times before. Their brain recognized the situation and started running the "meet someone new" program on auto-pilot. They expect a typical, predictable response like "I am a mortgage broker" or "I'm a real estate agent." Patterns, by their very nature, don't contain anything that stands out. They're hardly listening. They're busy thinking about what they're going to say next, or they're looking over your shoulder at the more important-looking person behind you, or they're deciding what they're going to have for lunch.

That's why your response must break the pattern of thinking that made them ask the "What do you do?" question in the first place. Stay within the pattern, and there is an almost zero chance they will remember you. Verbally slap them, however, and their brain will be forced to decide that you're interesting.

I discovered the power of a verbal slap early in my career. I remember going to networking meetings and hearing the usual: "I'm a financial advisor" or "I'm a Mary Kay consultant." To keep the meeting moving, a time keeper would give each one of them the hook after their allotted sixty seconds. When it was my turn, I'd say, "I'm a magician" and *whap,* the entire room would perk up as if they'd been slapped. Often, the sixty-second limit went out the window and it would turn into an impromptu Q&A session. I always ended up swapping more business cards because my profession stood out as unique. They had never had a professional magician show up to their meetings before. The statement broke the monotony and grabbed attention.

At this stage of my career, I've noticed that people simply don't respond to "I'm a writer" or "I'm a speaker" in the same way they responded to "I'm a magician." It just isn't a powerful enough verbal slap. That's why, when I want to grab attention, I'll use a self-deprecating joke about being a bodybuilding champion instead. It's quirky. It's out of left field. It's a perfect verbal slap.

As for your verbal slap, I understand that you probably won't be able to use "magician" or "international bodybuilding champion." That's the point. A verbal slap only works if it's DIFFERENT. It's got to be something unique, something so totally "you" that they are forced to realize that you are a unique human and not just another "normal" interaction. I'd write this for you if I could, but I can't. Nobody can.

2. THEN ASK A PROBLEM QUESTION.

Once you've verbally shaken your conversation partner awake, your next goal is to pose a problem that you suspect they will identify with. This must be spoken as a question. Questions have always been, and always will be, far more engaging than statements. The problem question from my pre-elevator pitch is, "Do you know how email, texting, and social media have kind of taken over how we communicate?"

Some respond with a simple "yes," and some launch into a diatribe about how awful modern technology is. That's okay, I let them talk. Either way, I'm aligning myself with them against a common enemy. This is one of the most powerful rapport-building strategies there is. However, if there is any doubt that I've just made a new BFF, I throw in one last rapport builder...

3. GO TO THE "NODDABLE."

A "noddable" is an inspirational or wise quote that is so catchy and agreeable, it gets just about everyone nodding. People will agree with these so strongly that they may even let an audible "Mmm!" or an "Amen!" escape their lips. If you want to know if your statement is a noddable, post it as a text image or meme on Facebook and see if it gets a lot of likes, shares, and comments.

My noddable was: "We're more connected than ever, but yet…more disconnected than ever." (I know—deep.) For additional rapport points, try this advanced technique: pause after the word "yet." This allows your listener's own brain to fill in the punchline even before you say it. When they do that, they have ownership of the quote. A small part of them is unconsciously convinced that they thought of it themselves. Then when you say aloud what they're thinking, it creates a moment of "great minds think alike" bonding.

At this point, I've already broken expectations and built some strong rapport very quickly—and I still haven't even answered their question. That's coming next. Kind of.

4. FINISH WITH THE CURIOSITY STATEMENT.

This is where you pretend to answer the "What do you do?" question. However, your answer will only want to make them ask another question. Here's the simple formula for a good curiosity statement:

"I help/teach _____ (ideal client) to _____ (feature) so they can _____ (benefit)."

Mine was, "I teach managers the secrets of true connection in a way that gets immediate results." This is so much more powerful than "I'm a speaker and author." Also, the intriguing vagueness of "secrets" and "results" builds curiosity and almost forces the listener to ask some kind of follow-up question.

The hard work is done. Now that rapport and curiosity have been built up, you can deliver your true elevator pitch. If you can avoid making your listener feel like they're being pitched to, it can be almost as long as you want. If, however, you get the sense that it's turning into a commercial instead of a conversation, then you're doing it wrong. Stop pitching and ask another question. Like most influence situations, you should only be doing between 15-20 percent of the talking.

There you have it. A four-step plan for instantly breaking monotony, building rapport, generating interest, and engaging your ideal clients in conversation.

The problem is, you can't use it unless they ask what you do. That's kind of like the new karate student who is well-prepared to win any street fight, as long as it starts with the other guy grabbing his left wrist. The next chapter will give you a technique you can use in just about any situation.

A SNEAKY TRICK FOR WHEN THEY TUNE YOU OUT

Everyone's brain has a bouncer—a big burly software program that either lets stuff in or kicks stuff out.

If you want your message to "stick" with your employees or your customers or your children, then you've got to get it past the bouncer. Otherwise, they'll tune you out.

Here's how…

Verbal disguises.

Look, there's just too much going on in the world. Every moment is a cacophony of sounds, smells, colors, and sensations. If our brains focused on all of them, we'd short-circuit. The brain's bouncer is there to keep out the unimportant details so we can focus on the important ones.

What types of things does the bouncer think are important? Movement, sudden loud noises, food, beautiful people, stories, our own names, and a few others.

The one technique that is guaranteed to get you by the bouncer every time? *Defamiliarization.*

The unfamiliar, the bizarre, the strange, the new. Novelty piques our brain's interest like nothing else. (Which is exactly why advertisers use and abuse the word "NEW!" so often.) How can you and I use the idea of defamiliarization as a verbal disguise to get past the brain's bouncer when someone is apt to tune us out?

Let's say everyone is sick and tired of meetings. Every time you call a meeting you're met with groans. Right before every meeting starts, people look like they're at a funeral. Their brain's bouncer immediately dumps that in the "not interesting because it's nothing new" bucket and kicks you out of the club.

So, don't call a meeting next time. Call a "gathering" somewhere other than the meeting room. Heck, go outside. It's a beautiful day. Just by changing its name (and location in this case) suddenly, the same old hum-drum meeting has just become UNFAMILIAR and therefore intensely interesting. They'll wonder "A gathering? What's this all about?" and you're off to a much better start.

You can get creative with this and make up a new term entirely! "We're going to have a quick conference room power-collab." This is another verbal disguise that will defamiliarize them from what they think they already know about you.

Too often in Corporate America we speak in the same old buzz words and catch phrases. The more often a word is used, the more it loses its impact. Our brains have learned to save energy by tuning out, ignoring, and forgetting the boring and repetitive. This is why you arrive at work, but can't remember how you got there. The commute was boring and repetitive, so your brain checked out. However, if something new and different happened—if you got stuck behind a parade, for instance—then you would most certainly remember that. When your words are like a boring, repetitive, been-there-done-that commute, your would-be listeners' brains will filter them out as though they didn't exist. When we feel like we already know something, we stop listening.

Speaking of not listening...let's talk about teenagers. Parents often ask me how to get through to a child who is shutting them out. They feel like they can't even get a word in before they are labeled a "nag," given the eye roll treatment, and bounced by the teen's brain's bouncer. How can you use this technique to communicate with a young person who is shutting you out?

First, try shaking things up by changing your approach. I like phrases like, "Hey! I have a surprise for you" or "Guess what?" The whole point of defamiliarization is to build curiosity and intrigue. Be unpredictable. Be a little mysterious.

Second, be positive. We can't let the bouncer regret letting us in. Are all our interactions negative (or perceived that way)? If so, then the brain bouncer will slap a warning label on your forehead that says, "Do not let this person in under any circumstances! They're nothing but trouble!" Instead, try saying things like, "You know what I love about you?" or "Good news!"

Once, I picked up my daughter, Sophie, from a play date. Normally, I was the last person she wanted to see in these moments. When I showed up, it meant that it was time to leave. The fun was over. She'd argue, cry, run away, flop on the ground, beg for a sleepover—anything but get in the car and go. I'd be left standing there like an idiot, embarrassed by her behavior and ultimately forced to be the bad guy.

Defamiliarization to the rescue. I showed up a little early and said, "Good news! You can play for five more minutes!"

"Yay!" she squealed. "We can play for five more minutes!" The two girls danced and giggled with delight at their good fortune. When the five minutes were up, she said her good-byes and thank yous and followed me right to the car without the tiniest objection.

Start as many interactions as possible with a positive note, an agreement, or a topic of shared interest. This builds up the relationship bank account and slowly but surely peels the warning label off your forehead.

One way to do this is to teach your kids to always say "hi." A friendly greeting and a smile can do wonders for getting interactions off on the right foot, but it is a courtesy so often abandoned with those you see every day. Add in the fact that we go through life staring at our phones, and we might easily forget to acknowledge and welcome people into our space. Throw in a hug if you're comfortable. Eliminating distractions and focusing on each other is a nice habit to get into. It's much better than jumping right into a to-do list or a behavior correction.

Finally, when getting past a teenager's brain bouncer, use more questions and fewer statements. "Get your uniform on" becomes "What do you need to do next to get ready for your game?" "You'd better go study" becomes "Do you have a test this week? Are you ready for it? Anything I can do to help?" The best part of this strategy is that questions cannot be argued with.

If you must impart some wisdom and questions simply won't work, then I recommend telling a story. In fact, storytelling is such a powerful technique that I'll spend the entire next chapter telling you a little more about it.

Here's the bottom line: every bouncer has a guest list. Either your name is on it, or it's not. Use the techniques in this chapter to get your name on the list so you can gain entry.

THEN, NOW, HOW: THE POWER STORY FORMULA

There is a lot of research suggesting that storytelling impacts influence. For example, Deborah Small at the University of Pennsylvania created two different versions of a marketing pamphlet designed to raise money for a charity promising to help hungry children in Africa. The first flyer was full of staggering facts, figures, and statistics, showing that world hunger is clearly a massive problem and you should do whatever you can to help. The second flyer also gave the facts, but it focused more attention on the story of one child, Rokia, who didn't have enough to eat.

Participants were given just one of the two pamphlets to evaluate. They were also given five one-dollar bills and encouraged to donate as much or as little as they would like to the charity.

Which brochure do you think raised more money? The overwhelming mountains of data, or the story of only one struggling child?

Those who had received the statistics-laden pamphlet donated an average of $1.43, but those who had received the story pamphlet donated nearly double, an average of $2.38.

Stories are an incredible way to connect with people. They can motivate and create buy-in. And there is no simpler story formula than "then, now, how."

THEN

Start by explaining what things were like then. Maybe the story is about your company, your CEO, another company, a celebrity, or even yourself. Ideally, the "then" you describe will resonate with the listener. It should identify a challenge or struggle they can relate to.

Example: Thomas Edison failed a thousand times while trying to invent the electric light bulb.

NOW

Tell them or remind them of how things are now. Ideally, this result is desirable in their eyes.

Example: Edison eventually succeeded, and now he is one of the most recognizable names in all of American history.

HOW

Once they've heard that positive change is possible, they're going to naturally be curious about how it happened. They are ready for your advice. Now it's time to give it to them.

Example: Failure is only failure if it happens in the final chapter. Now go out and find me a thousand ways that this project won't work.

The next time you find yourself trying to get your employees to buy in, or the next time you're trying to get your kids to listen, set aside the punishments and rewards for a moment. What "then, now, how" story could you tell instead?

The greatest influencers tell the greatest stories.

THE COOTIE WHISPERER

Everyone has cooties[4] in one form or another. To some people, you just aren't fit to be touched with a ten-foot pole. It could be for any number of reasons. That's the nature of cooties. It's a highly contagious made-up disease based on fear of an entire group.

Most of us vividly remember cooties from our early school years. The air was thick with it at the school dance when rows of young boys stood on one side of the gym and rows of young girls stood on the other. Cooties continue to strike fear into the hearts of pre-adolescents.

This is Paul Hughes's biggest challenge. Paul is a professional dance teacher with The Kids Dancing Program of Massachusetts. His students are fifth-graders, and the curriculum is seven weeks of ballroom dancing. Merengue, waltz, salsa, swing, and tango.

And cooties.

Lots of them.

---

4. For those outside the United States, "cooties" is an imaginary germ that school-children will pretend the other gender is infected with. I know that in the UK and in New Zealand, the equivalent is called "the lurgies."

The students start out as strangers. The first thing they must do is pair up with a dance partner of the opposite sex and get *really*, uncomfortably close.

"It was hard at first," said fifth-grader Stella Jarvis when a local television news program covered the final dance recital. "It was the first time a lot of us had to interact together, you know, not by choice."

How can you get somebody to do something "not by choice"? How is it possible to help someone overcome a deep, pervasive fear? What kind of influence sorcery is this?

After teaching over eight hundred students per year for over ten years, Paul says he has it down to a science. He anticipates the strong negative reaction that kids will have to ballroom dancing and uses the following techniques to transform the children from awkward tweens into perfect little ladies and gentlemen.

ACTING "AS IF"

The first thing he does is teach the students about posture and etiquette. No dancing. No touching. Yet. He has them imagine themselves as accomplished dancers and confident young ladies and gentlemen and asks them carry themselves as if they were.

The more they act with confidence, the more likely they are to feel confident. The more confident they feel, the less likely they are to be afraid of cooties. *Stand up straight? I can do that.*

What they don't know is that imagining and pretending are no different to the brain than doing. By acting "as if," they're gaining what might as well be real experience. By standing tall, their bodies are sending confidence signals to their brains.

EXPOSURE THERAPY

Paul doesn't rush them. He also doesn't let them go at their own pace. If he did that, then the seven weeks would come and go with absolutely no contact made. Instead he manages to have them in a waltzing embrace within the first two classes.

First, the students learn the dance steps alone, facing their partners about ten or fifteen feet apart. Then they bow and curtsy. Then they shake hands. Little by little they accumulate small victories over their fear. Before they know it, the chasm between the young boys and young girls is closed.

A series of small steps is always easier than a huge leap.

COMFORT-ZONE IMAGERY

When teaching the first dance step, Paul calls to mind an image. "You know when you're at the movies and you find an open seat in the middle of the row? You have to shimmy your way past everyone. Oops! You forgot the popcorn. Shimmy back the other way now. Excuse me, pardon me, coming through..." The kids get it. Light bulbs go off and the shimmies begin amid a series of giggles. "Before they know it," he says, "they are dancing the basic step in the merengue." The world of ballroom dancing has gone from a foreign landscape to a familiar territory in a matter of moments.

Later, when the boys and girls need to press their palms to their partners', Paul senses their cootie alarms on high alert and says, "You're not holding hands, it's just a high-five that stuck."

Great teachers (and great influencers) are masters at using analogy to compare new and scary concepts to old familiar ones.

BELIEF

Paul Hughes believes in his process. It has been successful for him in the past, and he knows it will be successful in the future. That's the thing with effective techniques. They work. Even when a new class comes through. Even when times change. You can count on them. In fact, some studies show that the more you believe in a technique, the more likely it is to work. If there is a student who isn't grasping something, Paul doesn't panic. He trusts his proven process instead of jumping ship.

Knowing that he has effective techniques in his back pocket transforms the daunting challenge of influencing fifth-graders. It becomes a game he eagerly anticipates. "I love seeing how they're so very reluctant at the beginning and, without them realizing it, they are changing."

Paul not only believes in his process, he believes in his purpose. His enthusiasm is contagious, and it motivates the students. He believes the benefits of dance go far beyond just learning the steps. "Dancing teaches, imparts, or instills valuable social and life skills," he says. And his belief is not misplaced.

Young Stella Jarvis agrees. Even though she was forced to interact with others "not by choice," at the end of the class she said, "After a while, we all kind of learned to get over it, and I think a lot of us became better friends."

THREE WORDS THAT COULD SAVE YOUR BUSINESS (OR YOUR LIFE)

While writing this book, I've been on the lookout for situations where influence seems downright impossible. Chapters like "The Vegetable War," "The Cootie Whisperer," and "The School that Words Built" are examples. This chapter is about a kind of situation that is just as difficult to navigate, but has higher stakes—MUCH higher.

I'm a person who is far from physically imposing. During disagreements, debates, and arguments, I've always relied more on mental agility. On occasion, I've encountered individuals who would much rather use their fists. When that happens, I've got a decision to make. Do I stand and fight? Absolutely not. Out of the question. Do I obey the King of Pop and just beat it? That's not always possible. Some people get quite angry when you try to escape an argument before they've had their say. Trying to leave only makes it worse when they catch you. Instead, when emotions are running high and logic and reason have gone out the window, there are three words that I'll trust to save my skin. I discovered them on the playground, but subsequent research has shown that these words can be insanely effective when it matters most.

In July of 2014, a Comcast customer service representative received a phone call from a customer who wanted to cancel their service. It quickly dissolved into an argument. It later blew up into a PR nightmare for Comcast as the recording of the call went viral. Here is a small sample taken from over eighteen-minutes of the customer calmly asking to be disconnected, but the employee deflecting, distracting, and outright ignoring him:

Comcast employee
"Okay, so why is that you don't want the faster speed? Help me understand why you don't want faster internet?"

Customer
"Help me understand why you can't just disconnect us?"

After listening to the desperation in the employee's voice, you get the sense that Comcast beats their reps every time they allow a customer to leave. The whole thing seems so unnecessary.

Arguments like this don't only cause financial damage; they can also cause physical harm. On average, there are twenty-four violent crimes of passion every minute in the United States alone, which is especially shocking considering how many crimes go unreported. And we're not only talking about punches in the nose in the schoolyard. About a quarter of *murders* are committed when arguments escalate past the point of no return.

It doesn't matter whether the argument was caused by simple disagreement, ego, hearsay, fear, misperceptions, miscommunication, hate, unfortunate circumstance, or a combination of all of the above. If it's too late to prevent it, the goal is to prevent escalation.

How hard can that be? All we have to do is take the other person's perspective, right? Put ourselves in their position? Walk a mile in their shoes?

Easier said than done. In fact, over the last few decades, we've gotten significantly worse at that basic human skill.

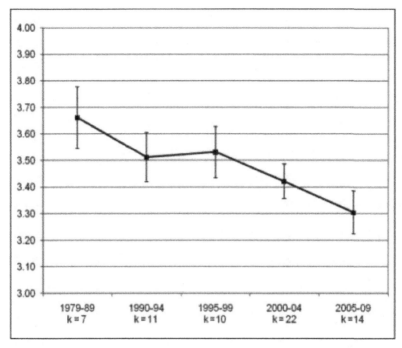

College students' scores on perspective-taking ability assessments by period. SOURCE: Sara Konrath, Ph. D., Director, Interdisciplinary Program for Empathy and Altruism Research, Indiana University Lilly Family School of Philanthropy

So, what do we do?

THE THREE WORDS ARE "YES," "THANKS," AND "HELP"

"Yes" stops the escalation, "thanks" changes the emotional tone, and "help" creates a sense of "we're in this together," preventing future re-escalation.

Let's start with "yes." Psychologically, it's very difficult to punch someone in the face when they are agreeing with you.

When we're in the heat of the moment, when tensions are high and emotions are charged, we MUST stop trying to prove how right we are. Instead we MUST seek out something that we agree on. It may take three or four tries, but if you say, "Yes, I understand," or "Yes, you're right about this," or even, "Yes, we obviously disagree" to someone enough, you'll be amazed at how quickly the heat of the situation dissipates. It's almost magical. Marital disagreements become calm and productive, workplace conflicts become about the issues instead of the individuals, and interactions in the bar or on the street are no longer deadly.

What holds us back is that we expect the other person to say "yes, you're right" first. We more than expect it. We demand it. I get it. It's hard to set your pride and ego aside. When you feel as though you're being attacked, the last thing you want to do is step inside someone's shoes and search for something that you agree on. But what choice do we have? The other way doesn't end well. So, let's resolve to be the *first* to say it.

If "yes, you're right" is hitting the brakes, then a simple "thanks for calling this to my attention" or "I appreciate your viewpoint" is throwing the conversation into reverse, taking you away from the cliff you were about to drive off. Thanking someone interrupts the anticipated negative pattern and interjects an element of respect for their opinion. This will also work on you. Just saying "thanks for your opinion" forces your brain to respect their opinion more. Just try being appreciative and angry or offended at the same time.

Let's add in "help" and give the Comcast guy a script that could have helped him avoid the frustrating conversation and the ensuing wrath of the Internet.

"Yes, I can absolutely disconnect your service for you. Thanks for being a loyal customer to this point. While I'm processing this, can I ask for your help with something?"

This assures the customer that his concern will be taken care of and stops the anger from building ("yes"). It begins to build a bridge of human connection by expressing genuine appreciation and acknowledgement of the relationship to this point ("thanks"). Finally, it re-opens the conversation by humbly asking for "help" now that everything else is taken care of. Once the conversational door is open, that's when the rep can ask some of the exact same questions he asked during the eighteen-minute call. He could retain the customer by reacting to the customer's answers instead of some pre-written script.

And this is where we see that TECHNIQUE is not enough. There was nothing wrong with the Comcast representative's technique. In fact, many of the things he said are taught in sales training programs all around the world as solid technique. The script itself was good.

However, the Comcast employee did not use that script in a way that considered the rest of the T.R.U.E. Hierarchy. In fact, if you listen closely, you'll hear a little Freudian slip that reveals the real problem at play here.

Comcast employee

"Because my job is to have a conversation with you, about having, about dis—I mean—keeping your service—about finding why it is that you're looking to cancel the service."

The customer service rep is clearly not focused on helping the customer. The customer service rep's REAL goal is right there in black and white: "keeping your service". In the employee's mind, it's not about a relationship, it's not about understanding the customer's point of view, and it's certainly not about doing the right thing and respecting the customer's wishes. To the employee, it's all about keeping the customer, and keeping the commission—at all costs.

I did some research, and it's no surprise that Comcast is making a classic mistake when it comes to motivating employees. Very simply, the more people who cancel, the less money the customer service rep gets paid. Ultimately, this is why the customer shut down. It's painful to listen to the rep bust out every sales tactic in the book while so obviously lacking relationship, understanding, and ethics.

Take the Comcast story as a cautionary tale. Just ONE of their employees lacked a full understanding of the hierarchy, and yet the results were devastating and catastrophic overnight. So, let's switch gears away from technique and have a look at the rest of the hierarchy.

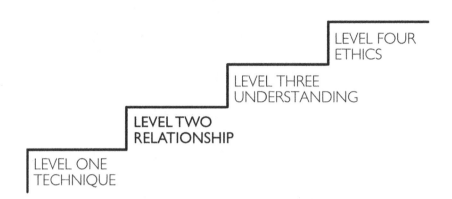

LEVEL FOUR
ETHICS

LEVEL THREE
UNDERSTANDING

LEVEL TWO
RELATIONSHIP

LEVEL ONE
TECHNIQUE

I just did a search on YouTube for "trying to give away money," and it showed me 26 million results. I watched the first four or five and saw what you might expect to see: people standing in the middle of a busy street trying to give away money to strangers. The videos may have varied in the amount of money offered, the location, or the appearance of the person giving money away, but what didn't change from video to video was the response. Virtually no one accepted the cash.

What's a better offer than something for free with no strings attached? Ask a hundred people what they want, and I bet at least eighty-five of them say, "more money." Ask a hundred people if they like free money, and I bet all of them will say "yes." So, why weren't people going for it?

Because technique isn't the only game in town. When you make an attempt at influence, people consider you using two different frequencies, the fact frequency and the trust frequency. If you offered me free cash, I'd use the fact frequency to weigh the pros and the cons (seems like all pros and no cons to me), but I'd also be using the trust frequency when making my decision: Who is this person? Do I trust them when they say there is no catch? Should I feel grateful or insulted? Will I be obligated to reciprocate?

Just about every personality assessment available today has questions designed to determine whether you are task-focused or relationship-focused. But just because you have a preference for one channel over the other doesn't mean that you can't tune in to both. Even the most hard-nosed, task-oriented achiever has a relationship measuring stick that he uses to guide his decisions.

If our relationship bank is full enough, I'll take a bullet for you, despite the fact that dying offers me absolutely zero reward. But if our bank were empty, then I wouldn't even let you give me free money, which is all benefit and no downside. Even though I'm a born "task person," I recognize that trust and relationship elements trump facts and data.

In this section, we'll look at the starring role relational influence played in a bus hijacking, a profanity-laced gym session, and the best bad job interview story I've ever heard. Even though the rules are completely ignored (or in some cases, intentionally broken), positive influence still takes place because relationship is prioritized.

THE AMERICAN WHO HIJACKED THE BUS

Wilberto Colon was driving a bus route he hadn't driven in years. He'd seen some pretty bizarre things during his twenty-one years as a bus driver in Boston. There were common annoyances such as obnoxious drunks, passengers who tried to evade the fare, and disrespectful people who played music loudly on their phone's tinny speakers. There was also the man who insisted that he bring his steaming hot bowl of oatmeal onto the bus—in order to feed his goat (The goat of course, was a stuffed toy). This, despite an official "no food" policy. However, Wilberto's route on Veteran's Day, 2015 started out calmly enough.

There were only four passengers on board when it happened.

While at a stop, a bearded and bedraggled bear of a man boarded the bus. Wilberto didn't notice anything out of the ordinary until the man said the words that no bus driver ever wants to hear: "Close the door. I'm taking this bus hostage."

Things happened rather quickly after that. Wilberto obeyed the man's wishes. With the door closed and the man still standing, the driver pulled the bus out of the stop and replied with a thick

Boston accent, "Why would you want to do that? You don't want to do that."

The man launched into a rambling and disjointed story about a lost job, family issues, homelessness, and what it's like to have nothing left to lose. Wilberto asked the man questions and played the role of sympathetic therapist just to keep him talking. It was working.

He glanced in the mirror at the other passengers. They looked largely oblivious to what was going on, just calmly staring down at the soft glow of their devices. Meanwhile, so many thoughts were running through Wilberto's mind. Thoughts about his life, thoughts about his family, but the one thought with the volume knob turned all the way up to eleven just kept repeating over and over, "*What do I do? What do I do?*"

That's when he noticed that the man had removed a weapon from his clothing, a hatchet. The realization hit Wilberto like a ton of bricks. *This is serious,* he thought. Then, and even more frightening thought. *What other weapons could he have hidden under those clothes? A bomb, maybe?* He didn't hesitate. He remembered back over two decades to his orientation safety training and secretly found a grimy button beneath the dash with his finger. As soon as he pushed the panic button, an alarm sounded.

"Don't do nuthin' stupid!" the man shouted at Wilberto. "I'll kill myself right now I swear to God!" He pressed the hatchet to his own neck and dragged it back and forth, causing a small amount of blood to flow.

So much for the "silent" alarm! Wilberto thought as his concern immediately turned to his passengers. They had all quickly moved to the back of the bus, as far away from the man as possible. One started banging on the window and yelling, "Let me out!"

Wilberto took a bold chance. He slowed the bus down and opened the back door, yelling for his passengers to make a break for it. The man appeared to be distracted, emotional, and distraught. He was mumbling incoherently, crying, but the hatchet never left his neck. Three of the four passengers got off the bus.

Wilberto steered the bus to a nearby intersection where he knew there would be a police detail. He and the final passenger frantically flagged down Captain Haseeb Hosein, the officer working the detail.

Captain Hosein called it in over the radio and immediately boarded the bus to attempt to defuse the situation. But the man's emotional state was worsening. Reasoning with him failed. Threats failed. Negotiating with him failed. Directly asking him to "Please put down the hatchet" failed.

By this time, a second officer arrived on the scene. Officer David Godin stood next to Captain Hosein and introduced himself to the hijacker.

"I'm Officer Godin, you can call me David. What's going on?"

The man continued scratching at his neck with the hatchet. "I know where my jugular vein is. I know how to do this."

"Nobody's doing anything here today. What's going on?"

"I got nuthin' left. Nuthin' good's coming around the corner. I been kicked out of the Veteran's Shelter. This is it. I got nowhere to go."

"Sir, are you a Veteran?"

The man gave a short nod in Godin's direction.

Wow, thought Godin. *How could this happen? How did someone who sacrificed so much for our freedom end up so down on his luck like this?* Godin saw images of the man's life story flicker through his mind. Battlefields, broken relationships, homelessness. It seemed an unjust fate for a man who gave everything for his country. *We look after our own* is the unspoken pact among officers, firefighters, and military personnel. But who was looking after this man?

Godin searched his eyes and said simply and sincerely, "Thank you for your service."

What happened next was described later by law enforcement as nothing short of "magical". It was a complete, spontaneous turn-around. Immediately, the man became calm. He surrendered the weapon, exited the bus, and walked to a waiting ambulance of his own volition.

The full news story can be found here:
http://boston.cbslocal.com/2015/11/12/
boston-police-save-suicidal-veterans-life

Why did this happen? What convinced the man with the hatchet to give himself up so easily after stubbornly standing off with both the bus driver and the first police officer?

It was the raw power of human connection—the most influential force on the planet. Godin displayed two specific components of strong connection, empathy and gratitude. The moment he switched from hostage negotiation tactics to a human connection strategy, he met the man's need to be noticed, to be understood, and to be appreciated. Needs met, problem solved.

In 1943 a man named Abraham Maslow released a paper titled *A Theory of Human Motivation*. In it, he described needs that go be-yond the need for food, water, and oxygen. When we need some-thing, we are compelled to do whatever it takes to get it. If we are hungry enough, we'll drop everything for a bite to eat. In this way, our needs motivate our behavior.

Eating when you're hungry makes sense. But what about becoming angry when you're hungry? (a.k.a. "hangry") Why do we get cranky when we're tired? Sometimes, when our needs are great enough, our behaviors become irrational, illogical, or downright stupid. In short, bad things happen when people don't get their needs met.

Dale Carnegie writes in his iconic work, *How to Win Friends and Influence People*, "There is one longing—almost as deep, almost as imperious, as the desire for food or sleep—which is seldom gratified. It is what Freud calls 'the desire to be great.' It is what Dewey calls 'the desire to be important.'"

Holding a bus hostage with a hatchet brings with it a certain feeling of importance. Having someone worry about your impending suicide brings with it a certain feeling of significance. These certainly aren't the best reactions, but they are reactions nonetheless. When Godin met the man's need with a simple "Thank you for your service," the man no longer needed his hatchet.

If someone is doing something you don't want them to do, then remember the lesson of the man on the bus. Find out what their underlying need is. Then meet it. When in doubt, assume their needs are to feel listened to, appreciated, and loved. In all cases, express genuine gratitude towards them.

THE TINY BUT HUGE DIFFERENCE BETWEEN COMMUNICATION AND CONNECTION

The story of the bus hijacker reminds me of the small, vitally important distinction between communicating and connecting. Get this wrong and your communication will never connect. Get this right, and an unfair advantage will follow you wherever you go. Unfortunately, most people get it wrong.

Attend any communications class and you'll likely hear a phrase that sounds good on paper, but this phrase can actually significantly damage your chances of influencing anyone. The phrase is, "It's not WHAT you say. It's HOW you say it."

It sounds great, but it's misleading. The first part is fine. "It isn't WHAT you say," that much I agree with. The second part, "It's HOW you say it," is where it gets misleading. The truth is, it's not about YOU at all. It's about what THEY hear. More specifically, it's about how they interpret what they hear. It's how they feel about what they hear. If there's anything I've learned from my first career as a professional magician, it's this: perception IS reality.

Every interaction with others is an opportunity to either increase connection with them or break connection.

What are some ways we can increase connection? Listening to others? Giving out compliments? Smiling more? Saying "Thanks for your service" whenever we see hatchet wielding hijackers? These all seem like surefire winners, but they're not. In fact, you get no credit in life for doing any of those things. Worse yet, as you'll see in a moment, you can sometimes be punished for them. You only get credit, you only get results, when people FEEL heard or when they FEEL appreciated.

Do you see the tiny but enormous difference between communication and connection? Communication is what you say and how you say it. *Connection is what they hear.* Communication, no matter how well-intentioned, sometimes misses its target completely.

This is a huge problem. What's supposed to work, doesn't.

Let's say you're in a meeting and you're taking notes on your phone. You're listening intently. You're taking notes. You're doing everything you're supposed to be doing. And yet, the boss gets frustrated and calls you out in front of everyone saying that you're "distracted" and need to be more "focused on the meeting instead of texting". It doesn't matter who's to blame. The fact is, there was a miscommunication. Even though you were listening, even though you did all the "right" things, you don't get any points for it because the boss didn't feel heard.

For those skilled at connecting, there is a relentless focus on the perceived experience of the other person. As unfair and unforgiving as it seems, nothing else matters.

There are countless examples of miscommunications and breakdowns of connection, but Officer Godin's story gives us an example of communication that connected. When he asked the man on the bus about his life, when he empathized with his situation, and when he said, "Thank you for your service," it wasn't just communication. Anybody can throw out the same phrase in an insincere way; it would not have carried the same power. We can say Godin made a real connection because (and ONLY because) the man FELT appreciated.

OVERHEARD AT THE GYM

There was a man lying on the decline bench, and someone who I assumed was his physical trainer was walking him through a difficult exercise.

"First, you're gonna do five reps of a regular decline bench press. Then, with your elbows locked, you'll do a sit-up. Then, you'll do five reps of a seated shoulder press. Keeping your elbows locked again, you'll lie back down and that will be one. You're going to do five rounds of that. Go."

The guy did fine until it was time to lay back down. Something gave out, and he crashed down much faster than he intended. His spine sounded like a bendy straw; I heard several of his vertebrae audibly pop in quick succession. The bar came down on his chest. If it weren't for the personal trainer's quick reflexes, the bar would have ended up on his throat.

After they managed to get the weight off the man and the man off the bench, the trainer asked, "What happened there?"

"My back just gave out. I wasn't ready for it."

"Well you're ready now. Let's go, try again."

"Nah, dude. I don't think I can."

The man sat at a machine with his head in his hands while the trainer paced back and forth in front of him like a caged animal.

"How do you feel?" he asked, without a hint of compassion.

"I think I'll be alright. I just need a minute."

"No. How does your mind feel? How does it feel to be a quitter?"

"What?"

"How does it feel to give up? What do you think your parents think of you right now? How do you think they feel about raising a little [whiner]? What about your ex-wife? It must have sucked to be married to such a little [wimp]."

The trainer carried on with his expletive-rich onslaught until the man got up and pumped out a full set with remarkable quickness. With a fire in his eyes, he threw down the weights in triumph and stood nose to nose with his trainer, fists clenched and muscles tensed.

The trainer returned his glare. I thought a fight was about to break out. Then, the trainer smiled, nodded, slapped the man on the arm and said, "Proud of you, little brother. Next time don't quit too early."

I sent my friend, author of *Actionable Gamification* Yu-Kai Chou, this story and asked him to comment. I specifically wanted his thoughts on how his Octalysis framework might explain what made the trainer's actions influential. Octalysis is Chou's map of the eight core drives that motivate human behavior.

Here's his reply:

> "It's a pretty straightforward "loss and avoidance" (Core Drive 8) that pushed this person further, with some "social pressure" (Core Drive 5) mixed in.

It's black hat, so it probably didn't make him feel good, but it can drive obsessive results. However, because it's black hat, he would burn out if that's the only motivation for too long.

The good thing about fitness is that if you do it, it brings out "accomplishment" (Core Drive 2), which is white hat. So, you thank the trainer. But if someone uses the same technique to push you to do what doesn't make you feel accomplished, then you might quit the whole thing early."

The terms "white hat" and "black hat" are borrowed from old western films. Directors would often put the good guys in white hats and the bad guys in black hats to make it easier for the viewer to tell the difference quickly. Black hat motivators are the "bad guys" in the world of influence technique. Intimidating someone with volume and vulgarity, even if done with the best of intentions, is most definitely a black hat technique. But that doesn't mean it isn't effective.

If you've ever been motivated by someone who told you that you couldn't do it, then you've felt the power of Chou's Core Drive 8. For me, it was when everyone important to me said, "Don't drop out of college! Being a magician just isn't a realistic career!" My desire to prove them all wrong, or more accurately, my fear of them being right, spurred me on to long hours, relentless practice, and high-risk/high-reward decisions that ultimately paid off. When Chou says that black hat techniques can "drive obsessive results," I know exactly what he means.

And it's not just ordinary people like you and me who are motivated by meanies. Many of the world's most successful were powerfully driven by a Negative Nelly. Just have a look at some of the GOATs...The greatests of all time:

He was cut from his high school basketball team, but if you ask anyone (besides LeBron James), then they'll tell you Michael Jordan was the greatest professional basketball player in history. He was the winner of an astonishing six NBA titles and countless individual accolades.

His teacher described him as "mentally slow". He dropped out of one school, was expelled from another, and the University of Bern rejected his Ph.D. dissertation because it was "irrelevant and fanciful". Yet we still consider Albert Einstein the greatest genius the world has ever seen.

Decca Records rejected them, saying "we don't like their sound, and guitar music is on the way out." EMI took a chance and The Beatles took their guitar music to the "toppermost of the poppermost," becoming the bestselling music group of all time.

In 2000, he tried out for the NFL. Here's how the scouts described him: "Poor build, skinny, lacks great physical stature and strength, lacks mobility and ability to avoid the rush, lacks a really strong arm, can't drive the ball downfield, does not throw a really tight spiral, system-type player who can get exposed if forced to ad lib, gets knocked down easily." In the draft, 198 players got picked before him, including six other quarterbacks. The very next year, Tom Brady won the Superbowl, a feat he has repeated four more times, becoming the only quarterback in history to win the big game five times.

At twenty-two years of age, he was fired for "not being creative enough." Fifty-nine nominations and thirty-two Oscar wins later, Walt Disney is widely considered the most successful animator of all time.

Her first boss told her she was "too emotional" and "not right for television". Her next boss told her, "Don't even try to beat [the competition], it's impossible." Weeks later, Oprah Winfrey overtook Phil Donahue in the ratings and went on to become the first self-made female black billionaire.

It was rejected twelve times in a row by publishers. Even when it was published, it was done so reluctantly. Bloomsbury only accepted the book because the editor's eight-year-old daughter begged. He agreed, saying to the author, "Don't quit your day job. You have little chance of making money in children's books." The book was the first of the record-smashing Harry Potter series. J.K. Rowling is now the envy of all aspiring authors, with combined sales exceeding 450 million copies.

Most would view these as inspirational stories of overcoming negativity, but what if the negativity wasn't a roadblock that needed to be overcome? What if it was a necessary ingredient to their success? What if the negativity was a gift? I wonder if they would have been as driven to succeed without it.

Sometimes an advanced influencer will temporarily don the black hat for a specific purpose. At the gym, the trainer's black hat influence led to the white hat motivator, accomplishment. However, if you ever plan on going over to the "dark side," be very careful. Black hat technique always comes at a price—relationship points. Can you afford it? Is it worth the risk? Be sure you've got a healthy relationship with the person to fall back on. Otherwise the relationship could be ruined—along with all future chances for creating influence.

It sounds like the two men in the story had plenty of relationship points in the bank. Even if they weren't blood related, the trainer used the term of endearment, "little brother," indicating a strong pre-existing relationship. Without a full bank, a physical altercation could have taken place and the relationship would have been damaged beyond repair. If the trainer continued to wear the black hat, then eventually the relationship point balance would be zero and the little brother wouldn't be able to take it anymore.

For some, there is a temptation to ignore relationship and just do whatever works right now. This is a mistake. Relationship itself is a powerful influencer. Earlier in this volume, I quoted my late friend Eric Paul when he said, "All things being equal, people do business with who they know, like, and trust. All things NOT being equal, people still do business with who they know, like, and trust." If someone has ever said to you, "Humor me" or "Trust me" or "Do it for me," they were tapping into the influence power of relationship. Likely, the relationship appeal worked when previous techniques did not. This is why relationship is on a higher level than technique in the T.R.U.E. Hierarchy of Influence.

Besides the influence power that relationship provides, it also gives you continued influence opportunity. A salesperson might not get the contract this time around. But if he maintains the relationship, he might win a deal in the future when the prospect moves to a different company. However, wasting too many relationship points on black hat techniques, or not making enough relationship deposits, can result in burnt bridges and blacklists, destroying any future chances.

With strong relationships, the door is always open.

THE BAD JOB INTERVIEW AND THE IDIOT SALESMAN

The job interview is the speed dating of the business world. A quick Google search brings me to hr.columbia.edu which says, "An interview aims to gather information about an applicant, present a realistic description of the position, ensure a fair selection process, establish adequate records in the event that the hiring decision must be justified, and determine whether the candidate would succeed in the position."

Unfortunately, it doesn't seem to achieve its ultimate aim very well—helping you choose the right applicant for the job.

Job interviews, especially unstructured ones, are no better at helping you choose the right applicant than tossing a coin. You might have more success if you threw a dart at a list of qualified applicants. Great interviewers don't always make great employees. Yet the ritual remains the most popular device for employee selection.

They're popular for the same reason they tend to fail—the relationship frequency.

Many hiring managers say that they would never hire someone without getting a sense of who they were as a person. Employers want to know if a new hire would fit in to the culture of the organization. It would seem risky to hire a complete stranger based on his or her resume alone. It would just *feel* wrong.

This desire to gather information, especially information of a relational nature, is exactly why hiring decisions often turn out poorly. Whether or not we like someone has no bearing on how well they'll do at work (unless they'll be working very closely with us). Yet because relationships are prioritized in the brain over facts and data, we tend to hire the applicants we like.

I know someone who was once on a panel to interview several candidates for a job opportunity. One interviewee stood out from the rest, but not in a good way. She arrived late, with disheveled hair, and she appeared to be quite flustered. Her words and mannerisms periodically struck the panel as a bit odd, but she got the job nonetheless.

Those on the panel said that hiring her just "felt" like the right decision.

In a similar story, I attended a seminar where a keynote speaker discussed his success and then offered a "how to" course on how to replicate it. His presentation was full of blunders and grammatical errors. At one point, he found himself stumbling. Literally. He nearly fell off the stage.

He didn't appear polished or professional in any way. His results spoke for themselves, but his delivery was borderline embarrassing.

When it was all over, more than half of the room RUSHED to the back table to buy his course. He was the top speaker at the event in terms of product sales and audience ratings.

This seems almost unjust. Doesn't proper grammar count for anything these days? What about punctuality? I guess people just don't value a good sense of equilibrium like they used to. So much for competency giving you an edge.

Why does this happen? How can a bad interviewer and an idiot salesman win the day? When does ineptitude become an advantage?

When it makes you *relatable*.

Far from being turn-offs, the job applicant's bumbling nature, grammatical missteps, and fashion faux-pas served to humanize her and make her more likable. I was told by one interview panel member, "You could just tell. She had a genuine eagerness. Her love of her craft was obvious, and she came across with such authenticity."

As for the idiot salesman, his mistakes led the audience to believe, "If THIS guy can do it, then surely I can." If, on the other hand, he was more "put together", there would be a sentiment of, "Of course he got those amazing results. Just *LOOK* at him! He's got it all going on. I could never do that." When an audience believes the secret sauce is in the person and not the product, they don't buy. Worse, when an audience believes a speaker is "too perfect," he is un-relatable, unlikable, and thoroughly un-compelling.

If mistakes make you likable, then why isn't this book full of typos? Why did I hire a proofreader to grammar-Nazi my manuscript? What's with the team of professional designers, typesetters, and photographers all doing their best to make this book (and by extension, its author) *look good*?

Because since 1966, scientists have been researching what Elliot Aronson first dubbed "The Pratfall Effect," and they have it down to an...um...science.

It turns out, not all mistakes and blunders are created equal. There are some specific conditions that must be met if mishaps are going to have their mysterious positive effect.

The first is quantity and severity. When it comes to incompetence, there's a fine line between endearing and infuriating. Some people's gross incompetence adversely affects others and therefore makes them wildly unpopular. Others are *always* messing up and as a result, they can't be trusted or relied upon. Mistakes are like a spice. If you try to make them the main dish, they leave a bad taste in people's mouths. Salt is delicious, but you probably wouldn't want to pop a spoonful of it into your mouth.

The second is whether you learn from your mistakes or repeat them. At the end of *A Christmas Carol*, we cheer for Ebenezer Scrooge when he throws open the windows and shouts "Merry Christmas!" He made mistakes of heartlessness and cruelty, but then he learned from them. Had he unapologetically bah-humbugged until the bitter end, I doubt very much that the story would have been as popular. There's power in admitting a mistake, apologizing for it, and making an effort to right your wrong.

Third, and perhaps most interesting, is the timing of the mistake. First impressions matter very much. If you are judged as being incompetent, then subsequent mistakes work against you. However, if you are perceived as able, then blunders will only serve to boost your likability. Remember, the idiot salesman had results that spoke for themselves. The job applicant's resume showed impressive qualifications. In both cases, their reputations as competent individuals preceded them.

There are other factors outside your control, such as the self-esteem of the other person or how busy their brain happens to be at that moment. By minimizing the quantity and severity of mistakes, learning from your mistakes, and creating a confident, competent first impression, you'll create an insurance policy that protects you from your future mistakes.

But how exactly to you create a competent first impression? How can you portray confidence even when you don't feel it? We'll look at that next.

THE BEST EMOTION FOR ANY INTERACTION

There's no question about it, there is one critical emotion you need to express in almost any human interaction. It doesn't matter if it's sales, leadership, dating, or parenting—without this single emotion you will NOT get the kind of results that you want. Period.

The bad news is that the majority of humans don't express it. It just doesn't come naturally for most of us, myself included.

The good news is that I know how you can *trick your brain* into *feeling* it. When you feel it, you'll automatically start to show it. And when you show it, science tells us that things will start to change for you in a big way.

It won't cost you any money, it won't take any extra time, and yet the results are downright shocking.

Ready to hear what it is (and my secret trick for hacking into it?)

Confidence.

Confidence has consistently been shown to be one of the most important determining factors when it comes to human influence. The problem has been that confidence feels like an intangible element—like it is some kind of immeasurable "x-factor".

Science has shown otherwise. Non-verbal communication, the *language* of emotions like confidence, is no longer as mysterious as it used to be.

The most exciting body language discovery, in my opinion, has to be "*embodied cognition*".

For a free video about embodied cognition and how it relates to confidence visit:
www.udemy.com/body-language
(Lecture #3 is free for you to watch and download.)

We used to think the brain was the command center of the body. It used to be possible to imagine a brain in a jar that had the full human experience (Think "The Matrix"). We now know that the brain desperately needs the body in order to experience a full range of thoughts and emotions.

When your body moves, it sends chemical signals back to the brain that affect how you experience life. You can't experience nervousness without the physical symptoms of sweaty palms, rapid heartbeat, and butterflies.

If you smile and laugh long enough, you will begin to actually *feel* happy. Even if it started as a fake smile. It doesn't matter, your brain still squirts out more happy juice in response to the position of your facial muscles.

So, the big secret is to **position yourself confidently**. When you do that, it takes less than two minutes for your brain to increase its level of testosterone (the confidence hormone) and reduce its level of cortisol (the stress hormone).

Stand up straight. Shoulders back. Feet shoulder-width apart. Open-palmed, symmetrical gestures. No unnecessary movements. Chin slightly tucked. Eye contact, and a friendly smile.

This position literally tricks your brain into feeling more confident!

It's crucial that you get this information into the hands of anyone who does any selling for you. It seems like a tiny thing, but if applied it has the power to make a massive difference in their success rate. MIT created a process that can predict who will win any negotiation with over 85% accuracy just by measuring the negotiators' confidence levels during the first five minutes of the negotiation. It's THAT important.

DO YOU COME ACROSS AS CONFIDENT OR COCKY?

"Where do you see yourself in five years?" asked the interviewer.

"I'll have your job in three," replied the millennial applicant.

This is a true story I heard from an attendee of one of my leadership seminars. Confidence is a good thing, but this wasn't confidence. It was arrogance. Needless to say, the applicant didn't get the job. In fact, the interview ended right there: *"Thank you very much. Don't call us, we'll call you."*

How can you have confidence without being seen as cocky or arrogant? It's a balance many people struggle with, and it's a challenge because most people have an incorrect view of what confidence is. They believe that a "confidence scale" would look something like the illustration below.

DOORMAT   CONFIDENT   OVERCONFIDENT

Without confidence, you're perceived as a "doormat." But if you have too much, you're seen as arrogant or at least overconfident. So, the key is to have some confidence, but not too much.

Makes sense, right?

Wrong.

This is not how confidence works. If you think my little diagram is an accurate view of confidence, you may be struggling more than you need to be. First, get the idea of "overconfidence" out of your head right now. Overconfidence doesn't exist; *there is no such thing as too much confidence.* Say this out loud until you believe it. The myth of overconfidence, and the fear of it, is the biggest killer of genuine confidence that I've ever seen.

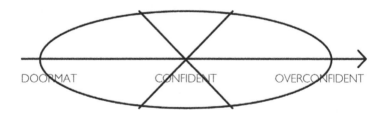

DOORMAT   CONFIDENT   OVERCONFIDENT

Confidence and arrogance are different things altogether. They are not related to one another, and you can have one without the other. Is everyone who is confident also arrogant? Nope. Is everyone who is arrogant also confident? Not at all. Bullies are arrogant, but deep down we know they aren't confident in themselves. That's why they bully others in the first place.

The opposite of arrogance is not a lack of confidence. It's *deference*. Here's another image to illustrate this concept:

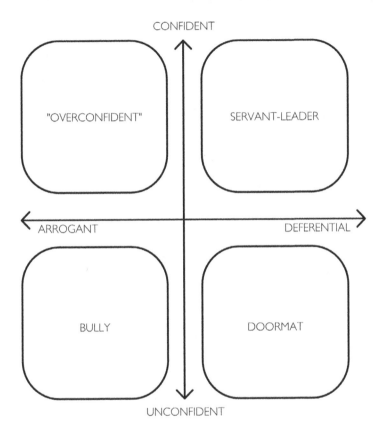

The vertical line is how much confidence you have, and the horizontal line is how much deference you have. Each quadrant has a description of how others see you.

You can have as much confidence as you please, as long as you balance it with an equal amount of deference. Without deference, you're arrogant (whether or not you have any genuine confidence).

As psychologists Adam Galinsky and Maurice Schweitzer write:

"Confidence and deference are not mutually exclusive, and it's usually a lack of deference rather than excess of confidence that gets powerful people into trouble."

Donald Trump, for example, appears confident, but not deferential. Lincoln was both.

The way to build deference is through perspective-taking. Seeing things from another person's point of view is essential. Had that job applicant thought about the situation he was in for just a moment, he would have thought about the interviewer's reaction: *"Have my job in three years? Hey, it took me 20 to get here and I'm not giving it up to some snot-nosed kid."*

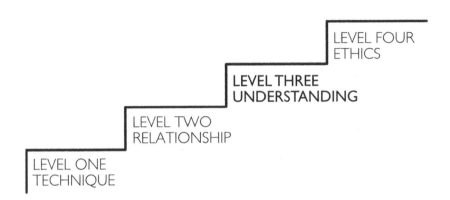

LEVEL FOUR
ETHICS

LEVEL THREE
UNDERSTANDING

LEVEL TWO
RELATIONSHIP

LEVEL ONE
TECHNIQUE

My grandfather passed out.

I don't remember the circumstances, but I do remember my grandmother's response. It wasn't the best of ideas, but it became an instant family story, retold year after year.

She poured water into his unconscious mouth.

Oops.

It's only a funny story because he didn't drown.

She wasn't trying to influence him, per se, but this story illustrates the importance of "Understanding" in the T.R.U.E. Hierarchy of Influence. It was the only thing she was missing, and the results were nearly disastrous.

- Water is good for you. On the whole, giving someone water is helpful. As a standalone **technique**, it's pretty solid.

- Their marriage lasted more than sixty years. Can't do that without a great **relationship**.

- In the moment, she was trying to help. Nothing wrong with that **ethically**.

Her technique, relationship, and ethics were on point. Can we just shrug and say, "three out of four ain't bad?"

Clearly not. I'm sure my grandfather would have agreed.

In the world of influence, the type of understanding you'll want isn't physical or medical. It's psychological. If you work with people, then knowing how people work will give you a strong advantage.

Unfortunately, psychological understanding of others is a rare thing indeed.

Right now, you're probably thinking that you understand others quite well. You might even be right. After all, if you're the type of person who not only buys a book like this, but also reads this far into it, then you're already a statistical minority. However, and this is important, *your belief about your understanding bears no resemblance to your actual level of understanding.*

The reason is simple. It's impossible to know what you don't know. The very definition of not knowing means that you are woefully and completely unaware.

The first chapter in this section will show you how your understanding measures up, and the rest will help you improve it. You'll get a glimpse into some of the inner workings of influence, but you can't gain deep understanding overnight.

That's why I invite you to join our community of thousands of people who receive my "More Influential" emails. I'll occasionally send you short, but awesome emails that help to increase your level of understanding. You'll get articles, audios, videos, interviews, PDF reports, quotes, stories, etc. It's a simple way for us to get to know each other and never stop learning. You'll look forward to them, I promise.

Join right now at:
www.MoreInfluential.com

WHEN OTHER PEOPLE STRESS YOU OUT

Read the question below and circle your response.

Do other people stress you out?

Always   Usually   Sometimes   Rarely   Never

If you circled *anything* other than "Never," then your level of understanding has plenty of room for improvement. "Sometimes" and "Rarely" are good answers, but life is too short to settle for good enough in this area. Any effort put into increasing your understanding of others will be worth it. There's no way around it, the opposite of understanding is ignorance; and ignorance is stressful.

In extreme cases, ignorance shows up as superficial judgementalism, stereotyping, and outright racism. But ignorance isn't always so easy to ferret out. Sometimes people's ignorance shows up in what they say.

"You people are all the same."

"Why would you do that? Why would ANYONE do that?"

"Women... can't live with them, can't live without them."

"Talking to you is like talking to a brick wall."

"You're such an idiot."

"I give up. There's just no getting through to you."

"Ugh, typical engineer (or accountant/lawyer/teacher/etc.)"

"This job would be easy if it weren't for the people."

Have YOU ever said (or *thought*) any of those things?

If so, then it's good news! Discovering and admitting your own areas of ignorance should put you over the moon with excitement. Your own ignorance can be fixed. Your own understanding can be improved. Which is more than can be said for other people's.

It's not that other people are all ignorant. It's just that you can't do anything about it. So, stop trying to fix the "who" of your organization, or of your team, or of your friends and start trying to fix the "how". The boxes on the org chart aren't the problem. It's the lines between them. The crazy people won't ever disappear. What *can* disappear is their ability to drive YOU crazy.

Imagine the person in front of you at the checkout is fumbling with her debit card transaction. She's not paying attention to the prompts, she accidentally cancels her first payment attempt, and then takes forever to type her PIN correctly. You're in a hurry and become agitated. A line has formed behind you. "Just go. I'll pay for all of it. It would be less painful than watching you try again yourself." You don't actually say that, but you want to. She apologizes to the cashier. "I'm sorry. I just found out my uncle had a stroke. I'm a mess."

Instantly, everything changes. She's no longer a bumbling fool. She's a human being who is suffering. Her little failures have a perfectly reasonable explanation. Your stress turns into compassion. Suddenly, what you were hurrying off to doesn't seem quite as important as it did a minute ago.

Ignorance is stressful and understanding is the cure. The deeper your understanding goes, the less other people stress you out. More importantly for the purposes of this book, when you increase your understanding, you increase your influence—and not just because you'll be more calm, cool, and collected. Understanding is the secret weapon of the world's best and most advanced influencers. Unfortunately, almost no one thinks to tap into it in everyday life.

The next chapter will explain how FBI hostage negotiators, mentalists, psychologists, and CEOs both expand their understanding and laser-focus it by using something I call the ITCH Bullseye.

HOW DEEP IS YOUR UNDERSTANDING?

Jeff Weiner, CEO of LinkedIn, says that the number one skills gap in America is interpersonal communication. I believe that the number one skills gap within interpersonal communication is understanding. Communication isn't about knowing what to say. It's about listening, and it's about knowing what people need to hear. When you have a deep understanding of people, then the right communication and influence techniques will come naturally.

Shari Alexander writes in her blog, ObserveConnectInfluence.com:

> "After interviewing the world's best influencers—including CIA field operatives, hostage negotiators, con-artists, and more—their first concern is never, 'What should I say?' Instead, their first question is always, 'What do I need to know?'
>
> All of your influential intel lies within the person you want to influence, not within yourself.

Master influencers are always looking for persuasive trigger points in the people they want to compel and convince. Figure out what is important to them. What do they want to achieve? What do they want to avoid? Observation is the foundation of influence."

I spoke to Chris Voss about this. Chris was a top hostage negotiator with the FBI before he wrote his wildly bestselling book, *Never Split the Difference*. As a hostage negotiator, his influence strategies absolutely had to work. If he failed, then people died. With all due respect to your top salesperson, Chris is the guy I want to learn from.

Before our interview officially began, I asked how one gets to become a hostage negotiator for the FBI. The first part of his answer wasn't much of a shock. "I got my undergraduate degree, I was a police officer for three years, I worked counter-terrorism…" That all seems like it belongs on the resume of a top hostage negotiator. But that's when he surprised me. "*None of that* was particularly relevant." Instead, the FBI's negotiation coordinator advised him to volunteer at a suicide prevention hotline, so he could increase his ability to listen to and understand others.

"There is no better emotional intelligence training out there anywhere than volunteering on a crisis hotline," he told me.

Ability to listen? Emotional intelligence? Is "understanding" really the secret weapon of the world's best influencers?

Chris explained what the first order of business should be whenever the stakes are at their highest. "Find out what their religion is. It's not necessarily the worship of a universal power of God, although in many cases it is, but what are the larger issues that they'll sacrifice everything in their life and be delighted to do it? Those people in Waco set themselves on fire—and a lot of them happily. If you can get to what somebody's religion is, you can get them to do nearly anything and they'll happily do it."

The lesson is clear. Do whatever it takes to understand the individual you're dealing with BEFORE you make any serious attempts at influence. Be a gardener, not a farmer. Treat each person differently and not like just another ear of corn among rows and rows of stalks. That means that as a leader, you need to know that travel incentives won't motivate Bill. You have to figure out that Jan's preferred style of communication is pure sarcasm. Don't talk to Jim before he's had his coffee and avoid discussing politics with Sarah. If you're in sales, get to know your prospects by asking questions and only doing fifteen to twenty percent of the talking. If you're a parent, take the time to understand that your children are each distinct individuals and they *should* be treated fairly, but differently. Doctors, lawyers, and teachers: learn about the patients, judges, and students that you deal with on a regular basis. Uncover their unique needs, desires, and tendencies. Get in the habit of being curious about everyone you meet.

Although understanding individuals will most definitely help you become more influential, it isn't always practical or easy to do so. Sometimes there are too many individuals involved and sometimes there simply isn't the time to have everyone complete a Myers-Briggs personality assessment.

Individual understanding will be helped by what I call "Tribal understanding."

A broader form of understanding is when we acknowledge cultural differences. Unfortunately, this doesn't come naturally. Cultural miscommunication can be a significant source of conflict. If you hope to sell your product into a new foreign market, then it would make sense to get some training on the market's cultural styles before you fly in for your big sales pitch.

Because this form of understanding is broader, it requires more depth. If you only have a shallow, or worse, an inaccurate knowledge of a group, then that could lead to stereotyping instead of genuine understanding. Combine a sensitivity to the nuance of culture with an understanding of the individual and you're two-thirds of the way there.

The broadest type of understanding is also the least common; it's the most difficult to acquire. However, when the stakes are high, I want someone who has achieved a deep understanding of human communication and decision-making. For example, it is unlikely that hostage negotiators, police interrogators, FBI or CIA operatives, or criminal profilers will spontaneously "hit it off" with the people they are paid to influence. Most people simply don't think like the criminally-minded. But if they are going to get the job done, they need to crawl inside the minds of their targets and reach a level of understanding that the targets don't even have of themselves.

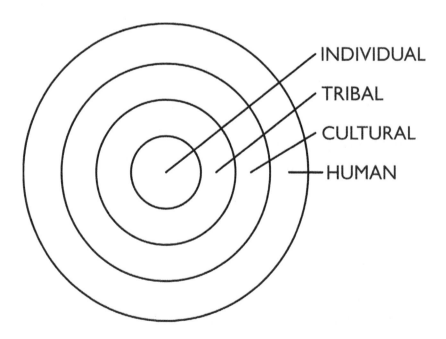

The good news is that recent advances in neuroscience, popular authors like Simon Sinek, Malcolm Gladwell, and Daniel Pink, as well as podcasts and even television programs like *Brain Games* are increasing our collective understanding of the human brain.

GETTING A "YES" DOESN'T MATTER

Three frogs are sitting on a lily pad. One of the frogs decides to jump off. How many frogs are left?

Think carefully. The answer isn't as straightforward as first-grade arithmetic might suggest.

The correct answer is three, because the frog only *decided* to jump. Nothing was mentioned about any real jump taking place. Isn't it true that there is a gap between deciding and doing? For example, consider the common practice of setting New Year's resolutions. A decision is reached on January first, and yet before long, the decision is abandoned. The road to Hell, as they say, is paved with the best of intentions.

Many books on influence teach you how to direct other people's decisions. Unfortunately, in the real world, you won't get the kind of results you want by only influencing their decisions. You only get life points when you manage to influence behavior.

Salespeople don't care about their prospect's purchasing decisions, they care about their prospect's purchasing *behavior*. Doctor's don't care about their patient's exercise decisions, they care about their patient's exercise *behavior*. Financial advisors don't care about their client's financial decisions, they care about their client's investment *behavior*.

In the chess match of influence, behavior is king. Changing a mind is like capturing a piece. It earns you points. It gives you an advantage. But the game is most certainly not won.

By understanding human behavior, we can reverse engineer effective influence techniques. This chapter provides a bird's eye view of the various factors that determine behavior. Some of these factors can be influenced by you, while others cannot. Some are fundamentally human, while others vary from person to person.

On a nuts and bolts level, behavior is directly caused by neurobiological phenomena. Neuroscientists study which brain structures and circuitry are involved in behavior. For example, the dorsolateral prefrontal cortex and the ventromedial prefrontal cortex are structures in the brain, just behind the forehead, that are hotbeds for conscious decision making. They gather input from other brain regions, weigh pros and cons, exert impulse control, and make decisions. Take the most famous case in neuroscience history: Phinneas Gage. Gage had his prefrontal cortex blown out of his head by a three-foot tamping iron propelled up a shaft by an accidental dynamite detonation. It entered under his left cheek bone and exited through the top of his head, landing eighty feet away (along with much of his brain). He not only survived, but he also never lost consciousness. What he did lose, however, was his impulse control. Before the accident, Gage was polite, likeable, and hard-working. After his accident, he frequently swore, gambled compulsively, and urinated in public without regard. His behavior was changed because his brain was changed.

A hundred years later, neuroscientist Antonio Damasio published his seminal work, *Descartes' Error*. In it, he described the effect of the emotional limbic brain on behavior. Before that, it was long-believed that emotion got in the way of rational decision-making. In order to make the best, most logical decisions, you should remove emotion and go full Spock. If you can't do that, people thought, then you're irrational, unpredictable, or just plain crazy. But what's truly crazy is trying to make decisions without emotions. Individuals with damage to their limbic system might spend hours deciding which cereal to buy, or whether to sign the contract with blue or black ink. They are completely paralyzed by indecision.

That's universal to all normal brains, and you can't change that. It's been shaped by millions of years of evolution. Understanding the part emotion plays will highlight the importance and effectiveness of using emotional appeals in your influence attempts.

Another area of continuing study is consciousness itself. So far, science has found that consciousness represents only the tip of the brain activity iceberg. For example, one study at the Max Planck Institute for Human Cognitive and Brain Sciences put subjects into an fMRI brain scanner and had them make a simple decision—press the left button, or the right button. The *instant* they decided, they pushed the button corresponding to their choice. A computer recorded not only the brain activity, but also the moment the button was pushed. The results were sobering. They will cause you to question your own sense of free will.

By looking at the scans, scientists know which button you'll push up to seven seconds before you do. Seven seconds! This suggests that decision-making is mostly an unconscious process (like heartbeat regulation or digestion) and your conscious self isn't notified until very late in the process. Again, this fact cannot be changed by influence. But understanding it will reveal the importance and effectiveness of what the godfather of influence, Dr. Robert Cialdini, calls "Pre-Suasion" in his book of the same title.

But the brain doesn't operate in a vacuum. While behavior is most directly caused by neurobiology, what factors are causing those particular structures and circuits to kick into gear? This is where human behavior gets even more complex.

What the brain does is largely influenced by what information is made available through the senses. The same brain plus different sensory input equals different behavior. A sudden loud noise causes you to jump. A bright light causes your pupils to constrict. Touching a hot surface causes your hand to retract. Not all of the brain's responses to sensory input are this obvious. The color red can make you want to eat. A warm cup in your hand can cause you to like the person in front of you. A smell of lemon can make you donate more money to charity. An effectively feng-shui'd room can make you feel relaxed. A slight touch on the hand or forearm might cause you to give the waitress a bigger tip. When there is music playing, you tend to shop longer and spend more money.

The senses are like testing facilities for the brain. As the brain receives new data, it adjusts its activity and behavioral output. The implications for influence opportunities at this stage should be clear.

So, we started with the most complex object in the known universe, the human brain. Then we added the complexity of about two billion bits of sensory input it deals with on a moment to moment basis. You can start to see why human behavior is difficult to understand, predict, and influence.

We're not nearly done.

Take the same brain, give it identical sensory data, and its owner's behavior can still vary widely depending on his neurological situation. Factors like stress, cognitive load, hormonal fluctuation, neurotransmitter levels, and other mood-altering variables will exert significant influence on behavior. This is a good segue into the territory of individualized influence.

There are seven billion living brains on this planet—and every single one is structurally unique. Brains are shaped throughout life by an individual's genetic makeup, experiential learning and memory, injury and illness history, maturity level, gender, drug use and abuse, etc. Your brain is not only different from your neighbor's, it's also distinctly different from what your own brain looked like five years ago. Any serious attempt at influence should include a thorough consideration of the individual or demographic group you are targeting.

Throw in the effects of cultural differences and social influence and you've got yourself a code more difficult to crack than Enigma. Our brain's relationship with our behavior? It's complicated.

Worse still, we've got lightning-fast technological advancements and rapid societal changes to contend with. A moving target is always more difficult to hit than a stationary one. The next chapter will take a peek at how technology is affecting the ways we communicate, and therefore, how we influence.

REVENGE OF THE WORDS

In 1960 Richard Nixon battled JFK in a series of televised debates. Those who listened via radio believed Nixon was the landslide winner. However, those who watched on television gave a significant edge to Kennedy.

Seven years later, Albert Mehrabian conducted a study at UCLA that would explain why. According to his famous findings, 93% of what we communicate is non-verbal and only 7% has anything to do with the actual words that we say. And with that, Dr. Mehrabian ushered in a sort of body language revolution. Books, coaches, and training programs started to come out of the woodwork. Every communication expert worth their salt seemed to be preaching the gospel of non-verbals. "It's not what you say. It's HOW you say it!" (Despite the fact that Dr. Mehrabian himself made it a point to admit, "Unless a communicator is talking about their feelings or attitudes, these equations are not applicable".)

Fast forward to the present day.

Texting. Blogging. Email. Social media. We are living increasingly separate lives that consist of staring at a screen for an average of seven hours per day. Kids ages 8-18 consume over four thousand hours of digital media every single year. To put that in perspective, there are only 8760 hours in a year and 4000 of them are spent either in school or sleeping. So nearly every waking minute is spent plugged in to a device.

When are they learning non-verbal communication skills? The sad answer: they're not.

Empathic concern is plummeting. Narcissism is on the rise. These are two sure signs that we're just not "tuning in" to others like we used to.

Blame the digital era. Blame Millennials. Blame an education system that is focused on standardized testing. Blame Big Pharma. Blame the president. It doesn't matter who's at fault, the fact is plain as day...

The face of human connection is changing.

Scratch that.

The face of human connection has changed. And maybe body language doesn't have the same starring role it once did.

I'm not sure what percentages Dr. Mehrabian would find if he conducted his studies again today.

The good news is... I'm not sure I really care.

Here's all you need to know. What you say isn't *necessarily* important. How you say it isn't *necessarily* important. Even the intent behind what you say isn't *necessarily* important either.

So, stop worrying about all that stuff. **It's not about you anyway.** Instead, start focusing on what people *perceive*. Rather than looking at percentages, we need to start looking at the overall effect that our communication has on the people we share it with.

That's so much more than communication skill. That's true connection.

That's the kind of connection that naturally leads to leadership, loyalty, engagement, sales, and customer satisfaction. That's the kind of connection that requires an understanding of your audience, an acuity for body language, vocal command, and yes, even (perhaps especially) a mastery of words.

John F. Kennedy went on to win the election in large part because of his ability to connect with his voters through a new technology. Technologies and trends may shift, but the person who connects, regardless of the tools used, wins.

A "REMOTE CONTROL" FOR BRAINS?

Recently, I landed myself in the hospital.

I had some abdominal pain, so they wanted to do a CAT scan. Pretty routine stuff.

It's when they started the IV that things got a little quirky.

I have no fear of needles. In fact, right before starting the IV, they drew blood.

No problemo.

But after the IV went in, I started feeling...fuzzy. A little bit faint. A little brain fog. There was a loud ringing in my ears.

Almost instantly, I was soaked in sweat. It felt like it was a million degrees. Then it happened.

Yup. I passed out.

My brain briefly hit the "off" button.

Afterward, as I lay on the stretcher, totally fine except for the embarrassment, the nurse told me I had something called a vasovagal response, also called neurocardiogenic syncope.

Here's why this matters to you...

BRAINS ARE IN CHARGE—COMPLETELY AND TOTALLY IN CHARGE.

If your brain wants to turn off for a moment, it will. As it turns out, there are a whole host of triggered responses like this that are completely outside our conscious control. (Obviously, it has nothing to do with how manly you are...)

It's as though there are buttons that control brain functions like consciousness, thoughts, and emotions.

Here's why "brain buttons" absolutely do exist and why they aren't going away any time soon. Your brain makes up only about 1.5% - 3% of your body weight. However, it uses about 20% of your body's energy. Thinking is *expensive*. Shortcuts are an absolute must if your brain is going to be efficient enough to be to deal with a complex environment.

When this happens, do that. Instantly and automatically. It's as though a button gets pushed and a program runs. No thinking is required, and energy is saved.

My vasovagal reaction was supposed to protect my heart by reducing myocardial oxygen consumption in response to an inescapable predator of some kind—such as a needle.[5] That's the problem with shortcuts. They aren't always accurate. However, the energy saved is a trade your brain is willing to make.

---

5. (*Clin Auton Res. 2008 Aug;18(4):170-8. doi: 10.1007/s10286-008-0479-7. Epub 2008 Jun 30. The origin of vasovagal syncope: to protect the heart or to escape predation? Alboni P1, Alboni M, Bertorelle G.*)

But what about a remote control with buttons to control other people's brains? Is it possible to influence the thoughts, choices, behaviors, and actions of the people around you?

It's actually impossible...

...NOT to.

Everything you do, everything you say, everything you DON'T do, and everything you DON'T say is basically mashing buttons on a brain remote. Your choices control the thoughts, choices, behaviors, and actions of the people around you.

You've got the remote. It's called communication. Like it or not, you've been pushing the buttons. The goal is to *label the buttons on the brain's remote* in order to connect better with the people around you and communicate with intentional influence instead of accidental influence.

WHY NOBODY LISTENS TO YOU

Ever have one of those meaningful sit-down conversations? It could be with an employee, your child, a client, your boss, your patient, or your spouse. They look you right in the eye and agree with *everything* that you say, and yet...they *NEVER CHANGE*. It's frustrating. It doesn't make any sense. What's going on here?

First, let me say this. I see this happening to everyone—parents, teachers, managers, salespeople, friends, spouses, public speakers, negotiators, law enforcement officials, politicians, and on and on. You're definitely not alone.

Also, it's not your fault if you're having this problem. You've just never been shown what it takes to *REALLY* convince people to change their behavior in a lasting way. They certainly didn't teach you this stuff in school. They don't even teach this in advanced management, leadership, or sales training.

That's why I'm so excited about the simple idea in this chapter. It's going to save you a lot of time, stress, and aggravation, and it will make you MUCH more effective at influencing people.

IF YOU'VE EVER TRIED TO CONVINCE SOMEONE TO QUIT SMOKING...

Here's the scene: someone goes to light up. You look disgusted and say,

"Why are you doing that? You're killing yourself. Do you know what you could buy with all the money you're wasting on those stupid cancer sticks?"

What happens next? Do they say, "You're right" and put the smokes away? Not likely. Instead, they usually try to explain their motivation to smoke. They'll say, "It relaxes me," or "I only smoke when I drink," or they'll provide some other reason.

Even if they do agree with you and put the cigarettes away, the moment you're gone, they're smoking again.

IF YOU'VE EVER TRIED TO MOTIVATE AN EMPLOYEE...

One of my consulting and coaching clients has been using a monetary bonus to help motivate their sales team toward a series of tasks. Very often, the message from management sounds something like this (and I'm paraphrasing...):

"Why WOULDN'T you do these things? They're EASY! It's like free money! All you need to do is do your job consistently for one month and we'll happily give you a huge bonus. You've got no problem with XYZ, and THIS stuff is even EASIER!"

If you've read this far, then I'm sure the results won't be a surprise to you. For the last two months in a row, not *one single person* has earned the bonus. Morale is down and the staff is now murmuring things like, "It's obviously an impossible goal because no one is achieving it."

In the case of BOTH the unmotivated employee AND the smoker, a perfectly reasonable argument (delivered with the other person's best interests at heart) actually turned into a powerful DE-motivator.

WHY DON'T LOGICAL ARGUMENTS WORK?

Well, let's think about it from the other brain's perspective. When someone is confronted with facts that are contradictory to their actions, they have two choices:

1. Admit that they're wrong (and therefore admit that their actions were stupid)

2. Ignore the facts and justify their actions

Which do you think MOST people choose?

The second one! Because of cognitive dissonance, the human mind will go to great lengths to avoid a painful hit to its ego—including clinging to wildly irrational excuses. No one wants to feel stupid.

THE "CARDINAL LAW OF PERSUASION"

"Never Make 'Em Feel Stupid."—*The Cardinal Law of Persuasion*

Read that again and let it sink in. It's kind of the main point of this whole chapter.

Making someone feel stupid for their actions sounds like a great way to lead them to change, but it only makes matters worse. It compels them to justify and explain their actions (no matter how frustratingly irrational those explanations are). It forces them to list all the reasons that SUPPORT their behavior.

Instead, you want them listing the reasons why they should CHANGE their behavior. People are ALWAYS more likely to believe their own words over yours.

So, when the smoker goes to light up, try this approach instead...

You
> "Have you ever thought about quitting?"

Smoker
> "Yeah, all the time. It's a filthy habit."

You
> "Still hard to quit though. Have you ever known anyone who's done it for good?"

Smoker
> "My brother hasn't smoked in 14 years."

You
> "I guess it's possible for some people. What made him quit?"

Smoker
> "He just got tired of it, I guess. Being sick all the time and wasting all that money."

You
> "What about you? Why do you want to quit?"

Your work is done. Just continue to ask questions and listen as they rattle off all the reasons why they should quit smoking.

By asking the right *questions* (instead of beating them over the head with statements and suggestions), you're allowing people to reflect on their OWN motivations for why they want to comply. Anything they say is going to be fifty times more powerful than anything you could possibly say.

INFLUENCE IN THE BATHROOM

For a long time, I've been interested in understanding how language affects the mind and brain. I noticed that tiny changes to the script of my magic routines would yield greater laughs from the audience. I saw how changing a word or two on the home page of my web site would significantly boost my bookings. I was fascinated by some of the patterns I discovered. I believe that understanding language gives us a glimpse into how the brain reacts and responds to stimuli.

The processing of language is considered to be one of our higher cognitive functions, but I've found that there are a handful of words that tickle the brain on a deeper, more primal level. Whenever a human brain hears them, there is a powerful and predictable response in behavior.

Since my book *Magic Words* was released, readers have sent me examples of those words working their magic in a wide variety of situations and locations.

Such as... in the bathroom.

After we use the bathroom, we (hopefully) wash our hands. Then, we likely reach for a hand towel (if we're at home), or a paper towel (if we're out in public) to dry off.

Some public restrooms however, have neither. They opt for an electric hand dryer. The electric dryer is cheaper than constantly replenishing paper towels, easier to clean up after, and better for the environment. However, because customers prefer speed and convenience; they tend to complain when paper towels aren't provided.

What is a business owner to do?

Some establishments give in and allow their patrons the choice of either paper towels or a hand dryer. Seems like a win/win. They receive no complaints, and even if only one person goes for the dryer, there is a reduction in paper towel use.

Others are more committed to eliminating paper towels from their restrooms altogether. They remove the paper towels entirely. Then, they try to eliminate the downside of hand dryers by introducing some kind of new "air blade" technology that will dry any hand, no matter how wet, in mere moments. Or they blow guests away by upgrading to overly powerful, turbo-charged engines that are practically strong enough to knock a train on its caboose. On more than one occasion, I've seen little kids fleeing from bathrooms equipped with one of these dinful monstrosities.

Magic words to the rescue. The best solution I've seen was in a restaurant bathroom that contained no paper towels and a medium-strength hand dryer. So far so good. What made it work, however, was an inscription placed right on the front of the hand dryer, nice and big. Anyone drying their hands would have been able to read the message.

If you were tasked with coming up with the right words to influence bathroom-goers, what would you put on the sign?

Would you try a simple, but polite message such as, "Thank you for using our hand dryer"? How about an appeal to logic, "This high-speed hand dryer is energy efficient and better for our environment"? Would you beg? "Please stop asking us for paper towels. We don't have any!" Would you lie? "Studies show that 92% of people prefer hand driers to paper towels." If you had a background in marketing and advertising, you might have it say something like, "For the ultimate bathroom experience, enjoy this luxury hand de-moistener, free of charge. Go on. Indulge yourself in the heat."

These are all possible techniques. This is why understanding influence is a powerful advantage. If *techniques* tell you what to do, then *understanding* tells you what NOT to do. As you increase your understanding, you increase the likelihood that you'll choose the best technique for the job.

It was none of these. The actual message on the hand dryer read:

"We use this high speed energy efficient hand dryer instead of paper towels because it's better for our environment."

Wait. Where are the magic words? I don't see a single "please" or "thank you" anywhere.

Real magic words often go unnoticed. In fact, I posted an image of the actual message on social media and asked people to identify which magic words made it successful in reducing complaints. Out of hundreds of guesses, only two people got it exactly right.

Many guesses were focused on reasons such as "better," "speed," or "efficient," but those appeals to logic are not the main reason the message reduced complaints. Let's unpack it using the T.R.U.E. Hierarchy of Influence.

TECHNIQUE?

Check.

Studies have shown that if you want to be more influential, include the magic word "because". In fact, it's so powerful that it can even work without a reason (Think, "Because I said so!")

RELATIONSHIP?

Check.

Using the magic word "our" is an appeal to the relationship level. It effectively communicates that we are all in this together.

UNDERSTANDING?

Check.

The intelligent and intentional use of magic words seems to indicate at least a basic understanding of human psychology.

We are part rational and part emotional. Psychologists call this "dual process theory". Effective influencers appeal to both sides, but they give 80% of their attention to the emotional brain and only 20% to the rational brain.

Sure, the hand dryer is "high-speed" and "energy efficient," but those facts are just sort of thrown in. The real focus of the sentence is the emotional and relational appeal, "because it's better for our environment."

ETHICS?

Check.

It's *true*. It is better for our environment. There is no deception here. This attempt at influence is an appeal to the customer's future selves. Sure, their impulsive, in-the-moment selves want the paper towels, but their future selves would prefer a cleaner, greener environment and the sense of contributing to something bigger than themselves. They want to do their part to help.

Not bad for one sentence found in a bathroom.

But it was not enough for Jos van Bedaf, the manager of the cleaning department at Amsterdam's Schiphol Airport. His problem wasn't paper towels. It was men who miss the urinals. As every frustrated wife and mother of male humans know, even an accurate but poorly positioned pee stream can splatter all over the bowl and floor. They also know how difficult it is to influence men to improve their aim. In some countries, it is a social faux-pas for men to stand while peeing. In America, there are some homeowners who make feeble, albeit adorable mess prevention attempts by displaying signs that say, "If you sprinkle when you tinkle, please be neat and wipe the seat."

Laugh all you want, but to folks like van Bedaf and his boss, Aad Kieboom, this is serious business. Take the minor inconvenience you experience at home and multiply it many, many times over. Consider the rows of urinals you see at airports and ballparks. Consider the crowds of men waiting their turn. Consider the effects of alcohol and/or enlarged prostates. And finally, consider what the inventor of the waterless urinal, Klaus Reichardt says about the males of our species: "As I have learnt over the past 25 years, bathroom behavior can be really strange."

The point is, somebody's gotta clean that mess. Somebody else has to pay for that labor and all the required supplies. Thank goodness for people like Jos van Bedaf and Aad Kieboom. And thank goodness they stumbled on a solution that, despite being a bit quirky, really seems to work.

I'm unaware of any empirical research surrounding their idea so exactly how well it works is up for debate. Some claim it reduces spillage by up to 80%, but Reichardt puts his estimate closer to 50%. Despite some hair-splitting, everyone seems to agree that it does in fact work.

Here's Kieboom with a long-winded and detailed breakdown of how a reduction in spillage affects overall cleaning costs: 'The total public toilet space [that needs cleaning] can be divided into about

20% general space, 40% for the gentlemen's and 40% for the ladies'. Of that 40% for the men's, only about 25% at most is reserved for urinals. The rest is for "closed" toilets, space for washing hands, and general walking space to move around in. So for the urinals, you end up with only 10% of the total space of the public toilets. So in fact reducing spillage by 80% results in a saving of 8% of the total budget for cleaning public toilets."

That's a bigger improvement than parabolic urinals that are geometrically designed to reflect all splatter back in toward the drain. It's better than ribbed urinals. It's better than mesh inserts designed to let urine in, but prevent it from splashing back out. And it's better than trough-style urinals, floor-level urinals, and any other gadget or gizmo conceived by urinal designers to slay their biggest dragon, the problem they call "splashback".

The 8% cost savings, however, isn't what caused a storm of media attention. It was the strange, juvenile-sounding idea of van Bedaf that captured the public's interest.

He decided to etch a realistic image of a housefly above the drain and slightly to the left. Why? Because all men are twelve-year-old boys, apparently, who are psychologically drawn to shooting things with their pee. "Guys are simple-minded and love to play with their urine stream, so you put something in the toilet bowl and they'll aim at that," says Reichardt.

That's right. You gotta understand your target market, folks.

And you gotta understand the three factors of splashback prevention: location, location, location. Despite the valiant attempts of urinal designers, the ideal solution is still guys just hitting the right spot.

An image of a fly seems to work well. It's something that is annoying and unpleasant, but not scary and unapproachable like a spider would be. Guys are happy to pee on a fly. But really, any image could be used. In 1976, inventor Joel Kreiss registered a patent for a bullseye image. While the idea of images and etchings in toilets goes all the way back to the Victorian era, Kieboom's idea seems to be the first attempt at using it specifically for mess-prevention with grown men.

Personally, I think Fenway Park needs to put the Yankees logo in every single toilet, men's room and ladies' room, urinal and otherwise. As a Red Sox fan, I know I'd be happy to do my part.

THE MOST FAMOUS SENTENCE IN THE HISTORY OF INFLUENCE

Abraham Lincoln did not win the popular vote. He only got about 40% of the votes, and some states didn't even put him on the ballot. He managed to scrape a victory thanks to a very close four-way race. But despite this unlikely beginning during a time of civil war, Lincoln went on to become one of the country's most revered presidents—and one of its best orators. His best-known speech is, of course, the Gettysburg Address. It's often studied for its rhetoric, and deservedly so—there are gems of psychological influence hidden throughout.

But there's good advice for all communicators hidden in just the first sentence. In that iconic opening line, Lincoln packs in four distinct psychological strategies designed to influence his audience:

> *"Four score and seven years ago our fathers brought forth on this continent, a new nation, conceived in Liberty, and dedicated to the proposition that all men are created equal."*

Tell a story. Research has shown that stories can be powerfully persuasive. In this case, Lincoln's now legendary opening is a little more specific than the standard "once upon a time." Regardless of his exact wording, these first words signal to the audience that there's a narrative coming.

If you need to be more influential in the boardroom, in the classroom, or from the podium, a simple story will greatly increase your chances of moving your listeners to action.

Begin from a place of agreement. Although he had to go back eighty-seven years, Lincoln eventually found something that his entire audience could agree on. Words like "liberty" and phrases like "all men are created equal" are pulled directly from a document that Americans—then and now — revere like no other, the Declaration of Independence. To nod your head in agreement at those words is a near compulsion.

It is crucial to get people to say "yes" to little things if you want them to say "yes" to bigger things later. So, start by acknowledging your agreements.

"Our." Lincoln used first person and plural personal pronouns like "we" and "our" both in the first sentence and throughout his two-minute speech. If you'll recall from the chapter on how to write an effective email, James Pennebaker's research suggests that these types of pronouns help develop rapport and create a sense of "togetherness".

By using "our" early on and peppering the rest of his speech with even more "we" words, Lincoln effectively gained positioning, status, and perceived confidence within his audience's minds. This technique, combined with the authority that comes with the U.S. Presidency, made the rest of his words much more credible and compelling.

Whether intuitive or intentional, it's clear that Lincoln stayed away from I-words and leaned heavily towards we-words, captivating his audience on a subconscious level.

If you want to improve your status and positioning, try removing as many I-words as you can from your emails and face to face interactions. Replace them with we-words.

Articulate a compelling reason. In the 1970s Harvard psychologist Ellen Langer discovered that saying the word "because" when asking for something increases your persuasive power from 60% to 93%—even if you don't have an actual reason. Unfortunately, that only really works for tiny decisions of relative little importance, such as whether or not you want to allow someone to cut in line ahead of you. Lincoln was dealing with a line being cut across a country. It couldn't possibly work with something of any real significance, could it?

That's why Lincoln used something that I call "Advanced Because Techniques," or "ABT". Although he doesn't state the word "because" directly, the entire sentence (the entire speech, even) could be summed up in the word "because". After all, just like any good "because," it answers the question "Why?"

Why? "The proposition that all men are created equal."

Why? "To see whether that nation, or any nation so conceived can long endure."

Why? "For those who here gave their lives that that nation might live."

Why? "For us the living, rather, to be dedicated here to the unfinished work which they who fought here have thus far so nobly advanced."

Why? "[So] that these dead shall not have died in vain — that this nation, under God, shall have a new birth of freedom — and that government of the people, by the people, for the people, shall not perish from the earth."

People need reasons to do things, and Lincoln offered more than one. His compelling list of hidden "becauses" etched the moment not just in the memories of those gathered, but right into the very fabric of America.

Figure out what motivates your employees. When they need a pick-me-up, remind them of those reasons. Stop pointing to the company mission statement. The only reasons that consistently work are people's own internal reasons. If your goal is to have motivated employees (or children, or students, etc.), then it's your responsibility to find out what those reasons are.

Lincoln became a great public speaker not only because he knew the right words to say, but because he knew how those words would affect his audience and compel them to action. He understood his audience's perspective. In order to become great communicators in business and in life, we too must be able to step beyond our own thoughts, feelings, and desires and master the art of words from other people's perspectives.

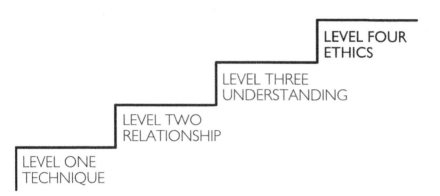

LEVEL FOUR
ETHICS

LEVEL THREE
UNDERSTANDING

LEVEL TWO
RELATIONSHIP

LEVEL ONE
TECHNIQUE

I'm not sure whether ethics can be effectively taught in the same way that algebra or history can be taught. But I also know that ethics can't be left out of a discussion on influence.

Some people believe that strong morals can hurt your chances at influence—that, in order to make a persuasive omelet, you've got to break a few ethical eggs. Everyone else is lying, cheating, and stealing, so you have to do the same just to keep up. Nice guys finish last, right?

Nope.

And that's not just a statement based in moral optimism. There is scientific evidence to back it up.

The following chapters will contain essays, examples, and experiments showing how ethical behavior turns out to be better for creating influence, not worse. Even in the cut throat, kill or be killed concrete jungle of big business, the same principle applies. It's good to be good.

WITHOUT THIS, YOU'RE NOT EVEN IN THE GAME

Quality.

It SHOULD be the obvious starting point. Nobody's buying into your solution if it isn't good. Whether you're selling a product, a service, or an idea—put time, effort, and resources into making it the best you can make it.

I realize that I've been caught on video saying, "It's not about being good at what you do. It's about being good at who you do it with." Being good at what you do allows you to *participate* in the game, being good at people allows you to *win*. I stand by the statement as long as those listening are already good at what they do.

At the end of the day, it's simple: make stuff you're proud of. Make it so good that not only will you want to show it off to everyone, but they'll want to show it off too. Good news travels fast. Unfortunately, bad news travels twice as fast.

We are wired to gossip. As a social species, our survival depends on our ability to trust one another. Break trust with one individual and that person will feel compelled to spread the word to protect the herd.

Without quality ideas or products, becoming more influential shouldn't even be on your to-do list. Simple idea. Short chapter. Don't miss it.

THE ANTI-GODFATHER MANEUVER–MAKE AN OFFER THEY CAN REFUSE

In the *Godfather* movie trilogy, the title character famously says, "I'm gonna make him an offer he can't refuse." It's tempting to try to craft a bullet-proof offer that can't be refused, isn't it? A perfect product that sells itself, a deal that is too good to pass up, or a no-brainer offer all seem like they might be the Holy Grail of influence. If you could just have that, then you wouldn't have to work so hard to get people on board.

Well, in the world of influence, there is a different "Godfather." Robert Cialdini is the author of the 1984 book that single-handedly revolutionized the study and practice of influence, *Influence: The Psychology of Persuasion*. Since then, he has become known as the "Godfather of Influence," and to him, making "an offer he can't refuse" isn't the best idea out there.

I was fortunate enough to get Dr. Cialdini on the phone for an interview. After our "official" interview was over, after he gave a brief mention of his newest book *Pre-Suasion*, and after he provided his web site for my readers (InfluenceAtWork.com), I snuck in one last question.

I'm including the transcript of the last bit here because in his answer, he reveals what he calls "another number one sales tactic" (besides Pre-Suasion, of course). If the guy who has spent the majority of his life studying influence tells you that he's got a number one sales tactic, then I think it's worth paying attention to.

Here's the last part of the interview:

Tim

Who inspires you?

Robert Cialdini

It's two individuals, to be honest with you, and they're not ostensibly in the sales domain. It's Warren Buffett and Charlie Munger, who are the greatest investment professionals of our time. They've developed this company, Berkshire Hathaway, in which they ask people to invest in what they have invested in, in the companies they have invested in. And they get people to invest in their company at levels of worth that are astronomical.

I don't know if you're familiar at all with Berkshire Hathaway, but—do you know?—like about a year and a half ago Google reached a thousand dollars a share on the New York Stock Exchange and everybody was running around saying, "A thousand dollars a share. A thousand dollars a share. My goodness." A single share of Berkshire Hathaway stock this morning is going for $245,000 a share, and they get people to continue to invest in them at those levels because of the salesmanship involved in their annual reports.

And here's—you know, if I had another number one sales tactic to advance, here's what it would be. On the first page of every one of those reports, before they describe everything that's gone well in the previous year they describe something that went wrong, a mistake that they had made or a weakness in their case, a drawback. And what that does is to convince readers—and I've been one of them, for fifteen years I've been getting their annual report—"These guys are being honest with me. What's the next thing they're gonna say?" I tell you it's so disarming to see them mention a weakness or a mistake, I believe everything they say afterward.

So, if there was a general principle, another one that I would recommend, it's that we know that in any case we have to make there are strengths and weaknesses. What we're typically taught to do is to begin with all of our strengths, and then, to be honest, we say, "But, of course…" and then we might mention a weakness: "We're a little more expensive than some of our rivals." Let's take that one, right? And we say that at the end.

That's a mistake. We're better advised to mention that up front and then to say, "But here's what we do to overcome that so that you will get a better value for it." It's by mentioning a weakness up front that we establish our credibility as trustworthy sources of information about everything that comes next. That's what Buffett and Munger do in their annual sales reports, and the results have been spectacular.

Tim

Wow. So, it's not the fact that it's—the technique is not necessarily honesty in and of itself, but it's that vulnerable honesty of admitting a weakness and combining that with the pre-suasion, putting that up front—

Robert Cialdini

Putting it up front.

Tim

—changing the order of how the information is presented.

Robert Cialdini

Exactly. Because when people are uncertain about you—if they don't know you—your best arguments are gonna bounce off a wall of doubt until they're sure that you're being honest. Well, mention a weakness that you can then destroy with the strengths that you have, and now they believe all your strengths more deeply when you present them. Remember that advertising campaign from Avis? "Avis: We're number two, but we try harder."

Tim

Right.

Robert Cialdini

That increased their market share by 700 percent in one year.

To get free access to the rest of my interview with Robert Cialdini, plus complete interviews with nine other top influence experts including influence titans like Frank Kern, Nir Eyal, Roger Dooley, and Dan Ariely, visit **www.MoreInfluential.com/sales-1.**

Honesty? Vulnerability? Weakness? These traits HELP to get deals done? By this point in the book, are you surprised?

If you were a skilled negotiator, you might be. I've experienced more than a few negotiations in my life (I have two pre-teen daughters.) So, I certainly understand the temptation to keep at least some of your cards close to your chest, particularly in high-stakes situations. The surveys confirm my intuition. I've seen studies that report anywhere from fifty to *one hundred percent* of negotiators conduct their talks at less than complete honesty in order to gain the upper hand.

Sure, your parents, some Doctor of Psychology, and an out-of-touch billionaire's investment firm might be telling you that "honesty is the best policy," but it seems like most people in the real world just aren't buying it. Could honesty have become passé? Was it too Pollyanna a perspective to begin with? Is it just a rule to keep kids in line? A rule that was made to be broken by "more advanced" communicators?

I wonder what Chris Voss would say about all of this. You'll remember that Chris used to be a top hostage negotiator for the FBI and he's written a book about negotiation called *Never Split the Difference*. Here's a negotiator who is at the top of his game dealing with life and death situations. You don't get more advanced than this guy.

I called him up and asked him point blank. He didn't waste any time or mince words.

> "Deception is a really bad idea. It's gonna catch up with you. It's like trying to play sports on cocaine or on steroids that are openly going to destroy you. It might give you a short-term boost of performance enhancement over a very short period of time, but then destroy you once you get out of the short-term.

> "In many cases, the cards you're most concerned about laying out on the table are the ones that are really critical to making a great deal. You could say to yourself, 'I can't tell them that if I don't get this deal, then I'm not going to be able to make my house payment.' Or the astute negotiator can say, 'Look, if you don't make this deal with me within this given period of time, I can't make my house payment and I gotta move on.' So, what you're hiding might be a strength depending upon how you pitch it to the other side. And in most cases, what you're hiding has actually got to be brought out into the open otherwise you'll never get as good a deal."

This isn't just feel-good, happy-go-lucky, Ned Flanders talk, folks. A top hostage negotiator for the FBI, the original influence gangsta, AND your mom all agree that honesty wins. These are the people I want to listen to.

Besides, I can vouch. I have personally felt the power of the anti-godfather maneuver. My first business as a freelance magician had me wearing a lot of hats, including the hat of a salesperson. I was the only salesperson, and I was responsible for every transaction. If enough people said no to me, my business would dry up and I wouldn't be able to put food on the table.

Unfortunately, a dangerous number of people did say no. When I got on the phone with a potential booker, after some initial small talk, they would always ask how much I charge. It was the first question out of their mouths. I would state my fee without hearing about their event or explaining what made my programs different. I had a ton of people saying "Thanks, I'll get back to you," but very few people doing so. Clearly, I was blowing it.

One day, out of frustration, I tried something different. "I'm happy to give you a quote today, but if you're calling around then you'll probably find I won't be your cheapest option." There it was. The anti-godfather maneuver.

People can be naturally skeptical of salespeople and will tune out at the first sign of being "sold to". However, when I openly admitted to my biggest flaw, it broke down those defenses. We were able to talk candidly about the event. I listened to the caller's concerns, asked questions, and detailed my offer. Before we hung up, she booked me.

One of my favorite examples of the anti-godfather maneuver in action is the story of entrepreneur and founder of the parenting magazine *Babble*, Rufus Griscom. Griscom pitched his business idea to investors by opening his presentation with a slide that said, "Here's Why You Should Not Buy Babble". Who does that? Virtually no one, which is precisely why it worked. The prospective investors lowered their defenses against the hard sell, because there wasn't any.

Their attention had been piqued. But not just any attention—positive attention.

When he honestly stated the weaknesses of his opportunity, the investors assumed that the list was comprehensive. While listening to most pitches, investors are trying to find reasons why the business idea won't work. In order to do their due diligence and avoid a bad investment, they shoot holes in every idea that crosses their desks. Griscom did the due diligence for them. Instead of shooting holes in his idea, investors were thinking about how to patch them up. He ended up selling his company to Disney, who brought Griscom on as a vice president and general manager of the business unit.

Any salesperson can apply the anti-godfather maneuver by flipping the script of their pitches. The laptop computer I'm using to write these words is one of my favorite examples. I was at the electronics store trying to decide between two models when the salesperson said to me, "If you're looking to get a computer, have a look at this one over here. The only thing I don't like about it is the hinges are a little flimsy, but it's got plenty of space and crazy processing power." Flimsy hinges? I could deal with those. I walked away from the computers I was comparing and ended up going with the salesperson's recommendation—at a cost of about $500 more. Oh, and by the way, those flimsy hinges have held up just fine.

Your marketing collateral could be flipped too. A brochure stating, "Five reasons to do business with us" becomes a brochure that states "Five reasons NOT to do business with us." I recommend that the reasons be genuine faults, but it can also be a tongue-in-cheek list (Reason #1: Our service is so good, you'll feel like part of the family. Which means one more holiday card you'll have to send out. Reason #2: Our prices are so low, your tax write-off won't be as big as last year's. Etc.) Why would any company DO such a thing? Because it is not only an eye-catcher, but it also builds rapport and trust. Because your willingness to publicly admit faults and reveal your personality creates connection. Because honesty *really* is the best policy.

Listen to your mother.

"BE AS CALCULATING AS YOU ARE GENUINE..."

I had just spoken at a large meetings and events industry conference. After the stress of appearing before about six-hundred of my ideal clients, I was decompressing in my hotel room. I had a now-defunct social networking app called "blab" open on my phone when a notification informed me that the author and popular blogger Chris Brogan was broadcasting live. Since I'm a fan of his work, I immediately clicked into his virtual seminar room. Of course, I wasn't the only one. Before long, Chris was holding court in front of dozens of his fans and followers. Chris is a master connector. There are several lessons we could learn from what he so casually pulled off that day. (Follow him at ChrisBrogan.com. He's good at people.)

At one point, I thought I heard him say my name. Now, I was still pretty new to the whole "blab" thing, but apparently the host could pull viewers in to actively participate in the broadcast. Sure enough, a moment later, despite the fact that I was lying in bed in a Las Vegas hotel room and dressed VERY casually, I found myself once again live on stage through the magic of social media.

After our split-screened, ear-budded faces engaged in a bit of small talk, Chris fired off an important question—THE question, in fact. He said, "Tim, I heard you once say that when communicating, you should *'be as calculating as you are genuine'*. What exactly did you mean by that?"

"Well Chris, thanks for asking such an insightful question. Let me start by expanding upon the…"

PAUSE

Okay, that's nothing at all like what I sounded like. Understand this; Chris is one of my writing heroes. What I actually said probably sounded more like:

> *"Wow. I can't believe Chris Brogan knows who I am!*
> *'Calculating and genuine?' Yeah I did say that, didn't I?*
> *Well… uh… sometimes you just want to choke somebody, right?"*

#facepalm.

No matter how good at people you are, everyone has their moments. Let's see if I can come up with a better answer now that I'm not exhausted, unprepared, and star struck like a giddy school girl.

REWIND

"Tim, I heard you once say that when communicating, you should *'be as calculating as you are genuine'*. What exactly did you mean by that?"

Great question, Chris! Yeah, I was purposefully being provocative by cramming two words together that most people assume shouldn't go together. Most people believe that you can either be calculating OR genuine, but not both. People who are genuine are nice, but people who are calculating are cold.

In reality, that's a myth. You'll get the best results with others when you are both calculating AND genuine. Let me repeat that. You'll get the BEST results when you are *simultaneously* calculating AND genuine.

BEING CALCULATING WITHOUT BEING GENUINE = BAD AT PEOPLE

It's the salesperson who cares more about commission than the customer. It's the lawyer who values a favorable verdict over the truth. It's the politician who loves the power more than the people. It's the teacher who prioritizes test scores over the student's education. It's the doctor who cares more about avoiding lawsuits than treating patients. It's the boss who demands unquestioning compliance because it's easier than fostering thoughtful engagement. It's the person who manipulates their new love interest in order to get what they want at the end of the date.

You may have flawless technique, you may have built a relationship, and you may even understand the inner workings of your communications. However, without the final component, without some kind of ethical compass, you are leaving yourself vulnerable to failure. This kind of calculated approach not only makes you a selfish person with questionable morals, it also makes you a bad communicator. People are quickly repelled by the fast-talking salesperson, the slimy lawyer, the bossy boss, and anyone else who tries to manipulate others for their own gain. Human beings aren't stupid. Our brains come equipped with some powerful BS detectors that we call our "intuition," "first impression," "gut feeling," or "vibe".

This is probably why everyone seems to be shocked when I continue to recommend being "as calculating as we are genuine". Let's not get confused though. Calculated communication isn't the problem. Calculated MOTIVES are.

You know what else is a problem? Communication that ISN'T calculated.

BEING GENUINE WITHOUT BEING CALCULATING = ALSO BAD AT PEOPLE

Maybe you prefer to just be genuine, to "wing it," and to say whatever comes to your mind the moment it occurs to you.

What could *possibly* go wrong when you're winging it?

Lots.

After all, I'm sure the father who screams profanities at his kid's coach is "genuinely" expressing his feelings. I'm sure the highly qualified job applicant is "genuinely" broadcasting her nervousness during the interview. Heck, I'm sure that sometimes your genuine self just wants to reach out and choke somebody! (That's where my mind was going with the "choking" comment by the way.) Just because it is genuine doesn't make it the best communication strategy. Clearly, ONLY being genuine is not enough. Clearly, we can't go around obeying our every whim all the time. Clearly, great communicators are also calculating.

BEING AS CALCULATING AS YOU ARE GENUINE = GOOD AT PEOPLE

- BE CALCULATING: Consider the other person's perspective. Deliver your message in a way they can hear it.
- BE GENUINE: Care.

So, let me sum this up for your viewing audience, Mr. Brogan…

We deal with so many different people on a day-to-day basis, and perfect connection simply doesn't happen naturally with everyone. That's why we have to make it happen unnaturally. In order to connect more fully with another person, we must push away our own normal patterns and behaviors and do something that is foreign to us. In other words, we must do something that feels highly *inauthentic. This brand of inauthenticity is far from a cold, calculating manipulation of the other person. It is actually a beautiful sacrifice.*

BE AN ADVOCATE FOR THEIR FUTURE SELVES

Tristan Harris, the ex-design ethicist for Google, stood on the TED stage in 2017 and said, "The only form of ethical persuasion that exists is when the goals of the persuader are aligned with the goals of the persuadee."

There is a question I ask myself to help me ensure that my attempt at influence is an ethical one.

"Who am I advocating for?"

If the desired outcome only benefits myself, then it isn't influence. It's manipulation. If that's the case, then often the communication deteriorates into some form of begging. Not very ethical, and not very effective.

And yet, a common question I receive from readers and clients is some version of, "How do I get someone to do something they don't want to do?"

The answer is, you don't. You can't. Not for long, anyway.

So instead, ask yourself, "What do they want? What do they RE-ALLY want? How can I help them get it?"

The answer isn't always clear, even to them. My kids would say they *want* to eat candy all day, but they'd get mad at me if I let them eat themselves sick. We've all binge-watched something for four hours straight because we *wanted* to, then got mad at ourselves for wasting all that time.

Imagine that I made you an offer. For the same affordable price, you can either have the picture-perfect, dream vacation of a lifetime, or you can have an ordinary, run of the mill vacation. Before you rush to make your decision, you should know that there is a catch. If you choose the perfect, dream vacation, then you will have no memory of it whatsoever. Of course, you'll have the time of your life while it's happening, but when it's done, your memory will be wiped clean.

Which would you choose?

Most would choose the run of the mill vacation. But why? A dream vacation is objectively better than an ordinary vacation.

Through a series of thought experiments like this, Daniel Kahnemann has theorized that our brain constructs two types of "self". One, he calls the "experiencing self," and the other he calls the "remembering self". You'd likely choose the run of the mill vacation because it benefits your remembering self. This choice illustrates our ultimate preference for things that benefit our remembering selves.

While pleasure is determined in the moment, by the experiencing self, true happiness and fulfillment are determined reflectively, by the remembering self. "How do you feel?" is a question aimed at the experiencing self while, "Are you happy and successful in your life?" is aimed at the remembering self. Most would agree that true happiness and success are more important than a fleeting feeling, but yet the in-the-moment experiencing self seems to take over when people decide on their behaviors and actions.

My experiencing self wants the chocolate cake, but my remembering self doesn't want the calories. Often, the experiencing self wins and we stuff our faces. My remembering self wants to retire early, but my experiencing self doesn't want to give up golfing money for an investment in a 401K. Often, the experiencing self wins and we indulge ourselves in brand new clubs. My remembering self wants a muscular body, but my experiencing self doesn't want to sweat and strain for hours at the gym. Often, the experiencing self wins and we stay home and eat cupcakes. My experiencing self wants the fancy car, but my remembering self doesn't want the huge payment and poor gas mileage. Often, we spend more than we can afford at the car dealership—all to appease that pesky experiencing self.

So, which one do we *really* want? The chocolate cake now, or the girlish figure later? We can't consistently have both.

While remembering-self benefits are sweeter, they require willpower to overcome the impulsive pull of now. Every one of these future benefits is on the other side of a sacrifice in the present. This is why we admire those who manage to break free of the desires of the experiencing self and achieve the higher benefits of the remembering self. It's the single mom who works two jobs to support her kids. It's the marathon runner who trains long hours. It's the bestselling novelist who honed her craft only after years of burning the midnight oil. It's the dieter who lost over a hundred pounds. It's the athlete who sacrificed a multi-million dollar NFL contract to serve their country overseas. These are people we respect, even idolize. These are people we are inspired to emulate.

On the flipside, it can be heartbreaking to watch those you love continue to settle for experiencing-self benefits instead of remembering-self benefits. Gambling, drugs, alcohol, fatty foods, video games, illicit sexual affairs, social media binges, retail therapy, pornography, or even the safety of a comfort zone tightly controlled by fear can all rob them of remembering-self joy and happiness to varying degrees. Some people manage to integrate guilty pleasures into their lives alongside the activities that lead to remembering-self benefits, but others are completely seduced by the moment and end up exchanging inner happiness for temporary pleasure. This is a common trap.

When your experiencing self says, "Come on, live a little!" your remembering self is hoping that you instead choose to live a lot. It hopes you earn the long-term benefits of deep relationships, emotionally-salient experiences and memories, good health, personal autonomy, financial security, and purposeful achievement by sacrificing the short-term benefits to the experiencing self.

My dad always said, "Everybody wants to get to Heaven, nobody wants to die." Malcolm Gladwell famously said that it takes 10,000 hours of practice before you can enjoy the success that comes with proficiency. The musician Prince echoed this sentiment with, "Sometimes it takes years for a person to become an overnight success." If you want two marshmallows instead of one, you've got to deny the devil on your shoulder.

According to a Native American legend, the grandfather said to his young grandson, "There are two wolves that live within every man. One fights for good, and the other for evil."

"Which one wins?" asks the boy.

"Whichever one you feed," the wise man answered.

For thousands of years, this has been a common theme around which many of our literature's most enduring stories have been written. They warn against "selling your soul" and advocate for the wisdom of forward-thinking decisions. Imagine that the devil on one shoulder is an advocate for your experiencing self and the angel on the other is an advocate for your remembering self. It's not a battle between good and evil. It's a battle between good and less good.

Ethical influence encourages and advocates for the remembering selves of others. Feed their good wolf.

It's the salesperson who gets their prospect to overcome their short-term fear of spending a few extra dollars so they can enjoy the long-term benefits that come with a wise investment decision.

It's the parent who gets their teenage child to sacrifice the in-the-moment pleasure of drugs and alcohol so they can enjoy long and happy lives free of substance dependence and regret.

It's the doctor who gets their young patient to endure the in-the-moment pain of a shot for the long-term benefits of immunization.

It's the teacher who encourages their students to forego a portion of the fun that television and video games provide to create more time for the long-term brain benefits of reading.

And it's the father who holds his daughter down and forces her to pierce her ears.

Um, I think we're going to need some context on that last one.

CHILD ABUSE OR FATHER OF THE YEAR?

One of my daughters wanted to pierce her ears. She had been thinking about it for some time, and when her sister got hers done, it became a pressing matter of importance. The two of us headed to the mall to pick out her first set of earrings and have them installed.

So far so good. The kid was happy and excited until it came time to sit in the chair. Once the two gloved employees got into her personal space, she freaked. There was a panicked scream, a lightning-fast exit, and an urgent sprint down the tiled corridor towards the padded play place.

A bit surprised, I watched her put some distance between us before I realized that she wasn't coming back. "Sorry," I said to the store clerks, who were both sporting "here we go again" faces.

I caught up with her, gave her a hug, wiped her tears, and we started back towards the chair. "You don't have to do this, you know. We can leave right now if you want."

"No!" she sobbed. "I want earrings!"

"Okay, okay. Let's go. They're still waiting for you."

"No! Daddy, it's gonna hurt!"

I couldn't make her happy. Her two selves had locked horns. Her remembering self wanted the earrings, but her experiencing self wanted to avoid the momentary pinch. It was a dilemma.

If ever there was an opportunity to exercise some TRUE influence, this was it. I knew how excited she would be once they were in. I knew the pain was quick and minimal. It was time to be an advocate for her remembering self.

The clerks were still holding the piercing guns, their sterilized hands up in the air, unable to touch anything unclean. They looked like disgruntled, armed surgeons.

I tried a few quick techniques to get her past her fear. I said, "I know you feel scared, right now, but what will happen if we get home tonight without any earrings?" The techniques in that sentence were *begin at agreement, disassociate from absolutes, presupposition, curiosity, "but eraser,"* and *anticipation of regret.* I continued with some *social influence* ("Your sister said she could barely even feel it"), *anticipation of reward* and *more social influence* ("Who is the first person you're going to show your new earrings to?"), and *reframing* ("Is it possible that the feeling in your belly is just excitement?")

All of this got her to approach the store, but then her brain's impulse control wavered and the urge to run took over once again.

I didn't give up. I believed that the combination of techniques and my relationship with "daddy's little girl" would prevail and create a happy ending. "You can sit right in my lap. I'm not going anywhere. I'll hold your hand the entire time."

Besides, now that the seal on those earrings was broken, I had to pay for them whether they ended up in my daughter's earlobes or not. Twenty-two dollars hung in the balance. Oh yes. This was happening.

The clerks were growing impatient. "You know," they said as a line began to form at the register. "You're not a bad father if you just hold her down."

"Okay. Give us a second."

Time was running out. I sat her in my lap and reached for an influence power tool: a "Then, Now, How" story.

"Once, when I was about your age, we took a canoe trip in New Hampshire. Where the water was deep enough, someone had set up a monkey swing. Do you know what a monkey swing is?"

"No." *Sniffle.*

"It's a long rope tied to a tall tree branch that hangs out over the water. You climb the tree, hold onto the rope as tight as you can, and then swing out over the water like a monkey. Then you let go and do a humungous cannonball into the water. Sounds fun, right?"

She nodded.

"I thought so too…until I climbed up the tree and looked down. I was terrified—totally frozen with fear. Everyone was yelling at me to just do it. They said it was fun and safe and that I had nothing to be afraid of. But that just made it worse when they pressured me. Kind of like how everyone is pressuring you right now, huh?"

A nod.

"Then, I didn't see it coming, but my brother pushed me. I held on to the rope for dear life. I didn't want to let go! But I had to. I splashed into the water and when I came up, I had a huge smile on my face. I screamed, 'AGAIN!' I did it about ten more times after that. I wasn't afraid anymore all because someone gave me a little push."

I let it sink in for a moment.

"Honey?" I prodded.

"Yeah…"

"Do you want me to give you a little push?"

She closed her eyes, squeezed out one more tear and nodded.

There. It was decided. I carried her into the store and put her in my lap. One of my forearms was low and tight across her waist and my other hand held her head still against my chest. I nodded to the clerks and took a deep breath.

When she saw the moment of truth drawing near, it got real. My daughter's eyes grew big, she bucked like a fish out of water, and out came a horror-movie screech, "DADDY, DON'T MAKE ME DO THIS!"

I experienced a mix of emotions, but shocked passers-by stuck to disgust. "Oh my God!" one gasped with contempt. Others just stopped and stared.

In an instant, it was over.

"That's it?" she asked through tears.

"Told you. Quick as a wink," said one of the exasperated clerks as she snapped off her rubber gloves and tended to her restless customers.

The other held a mirror in front of my daughter, and the smile I glimpsed reminded me of the one I made decades before in the mountain runoff stream. The pain of the experience vanished. Her remembering self was elated. The line of customers was smiling too.

Those walking past saw what they thought was a child abuser. Those in the queue saw what they thought was a candidate for "father of the year". The truth lies somewhere in between, but all that matters to me is that my little girl knows that even if he's holding her down like a Brazilian Jiu-Jitsu black belt, Daddy's got her back.

NICE CHAPTERS FINISH LAST

Think of someone who you personally consider to be influential in your life. Someone who commands your attention and respect when they speak or act. Someone who you might strive to emulate.

Evaluate the person you're thinking of using the following scale.

Is he or she…

	NEVER 1	2	SOMETIMES 3	4	ALWAYS 5
Reliable/Consistent					
Patient					
Available					
Caring/Humane					
Humble/Selfless					

	NEVER 1	2	SOMETIMES 3	4	ALWAYS 5
A Good Listener					
Accountable					
Honest					
Present					
Giving					
Informal/ Friendly					
Encouraging					
Interested in People					
Kind					
Has Integrity					
Respectful					
Genuine					
Trustworthy					
Forgiving					

No one person is perfect, but I would imagine you checked off a lot of threes, fours, and fives. After all, I asked you to think of an influential individual. It should be no surprise that an influential person scored highly on an influence assessment. Except...the assessment has nothing at all to do with influence. Not directly anyway.

I didn't choose this list of characteristics based on what makes someone influential. Instead, this is a list of moral qualities. It is a list of "character"-istics. I started by searching Google for general terms like "ethical characteristics," "good moral qualities," and "how to be a good person". (After all, what better moral compass is there than Google?) I found repeating themes in the search results and used them to compile the list of attributes above. Kindness, altruism, selflessness, et al. are stereotypically saintly. Few would argue that giving to others makes you a jerk. Experts from a variety of backgrounds seem to agree that possessing these traits would get someone labeled a "good person".

Then why did your influential person score highly on a test designed for measuring good moral character?

Could there be a correlation? Does whether or not someone is a good person predict whether or not they are an influential individual? Is it possible that their goodness *created* their cache and clout?

In his book *Give and Take—Why Helping Others Drives Our Success*, Adam Grant provides an answer.

> *"Research demonstrates that givers sink to the bottom of the success ladder. Across a wide range of important occupations, givers are at a disadvantage: they make others better off but sacrifice their own success in the process."*

There definitely seems to be a correlation, but hold on...did he say, "bottom of the success ladder" and that "givers are at a *disadvantage*"? What's going on here?

First, a little background on where Grant got his information.

First, he surveyed over 30,000 people from around the world and across cultures to find out if people are primarily givers or takers. Givers are the "good" people—altruistic, willing to help, focused on others. Takers, on the other hand, are more likely to behave in ways that benefit themselves, regardless of who they hurt along the way. Grant says it's not easy to tell who is who without the survey. We've all met people who appear to be a bit gruff on the outside but have a heart of gold. We've also heard stories of psychopathic serial killers who are charming and affable.

It's even hard to know where we fall on the spectrum ourselves. If asked, about two-thirds of people will self-identify as givers and only about 6% will claim to be takers. In reality, about one in five people are takers. There seem to be slightly more givers at about one person in every four.

It's good to know there are more givers than takers, but the astute reader will notice that something is amiss with the math. There is still over half the population unaccounted for. That's because the majority of individuals are neither givers nor takers. They fall somewhere in between. The people in this third category are what Grant calls, "matchers". They'll be a giver to you if you're first a giver to them. However, if you begin to take advantage of their giving, then they'll become a taker themselves. If "do unto others as they want to be done unto" is the golden rule for givers, and "do unto others before they do unto you" is the golden rule for takers, then the matchers' golden rule is, "do unto others as they've done unto you."

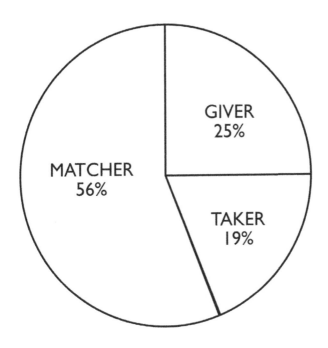

But is that a wise philosophy? It must be, if we've evolved to be a mostly-matcher society. But what about those who want to get to the top of the top? Matchers seem to survive just fine, but what if you want to do more than that? What if you want to thrive? Should you be a matcher or a taker? Again, Grant has the answer.

"So, if givers are most likely to land at the bottom of the success ladder, who's at the top—takers or matchers? Neither. When I took another look at the data, I discovered a surprising pattern: It's the givers again."

Taking is certainly effective in the short term. You can absolutely use manipulative marketing and sales techniques to get a customer to buy. You can most certainly convince a previously unwilling romantic partner to spend the night with you. You can negotiate favorable deals, persuade voters, control students, trick donors, and on and on. So why don't takers jump straight to the top of the success ladder?

It's because of the matching majority. When matchers sniff out a taker, they will do everything in their power to bring them down a peg—even if it comes at a personal cost to the matcher. Their sense of fairness can outweigh their desire to gain.

This can be demonstrated powerfully with the psychology professor's favorite in-classroom demonstration, the "ultimatum game". The game is played in groups of two. The first participant is given something of value, say, ten dollars, and asked to keep some for himself and offer the rest to the second participant. The participant can keep nine or ten dollars for himself if he so desires, but there's a catch. The second participant must accept the offer. If the offer is rejected, then both participants walk away with nothing.

No discussion is allowed before the offer is made, and no counteroffers are permitted. Hence the name, "The Ultimatum Game".

What would you do?

A taker might offer between one and three dollars to his partner, attempting to maximize his own portion. A giver might offer his partner five to seven dollars, instead choosing to maximize the chance that the offer is accepted. The offer tendencies however, are not nearly as interesting as the rejection tendencies.

Offers as high as three dollars are routinely rejected.

Why would anyone *ever* say no in this game? It's free money! Why should it matter what the other person is getting? Even the smallest offer is better than zero, right?

If money and self-interest were the only things that mattered, then yes. It would be. But in this game, there's another force at play—our sense of fairness. Matchers (most people) would rather lose than allow an unfair offer to go unchecked.

When takers win at the game of life, we feel jealousy and a little bit of anger. Matchers and other takers seek to correct the balance of justice in the universe by knocking down those takers. It may take time, but what goes around tends to come around. When givers win, however, it's only the takers who are seeking to tear them down. The other eighty-one percent of the population is lifting the givers up and cheering them on, making them even more successful.

Grant concludes succinctly, "Being a giver is not good for a 100-yard dash, but it's valuable in a marathon."

Grant isn't the first to come to that realization. In the early 1980s, political scientist Robert Axelrod and evolutionary biologist William Hamilton made up the unlikely team that revolutionized how we think about the benefits of cooperation.

Why would anyone ever play nice if they can instead maximize their own lot in life by lying, cheating, and stealing? Why share if you can keep it all to yourself? Where the heck did selfless altruism *come from*? Axelrod's 1984 book *The Evolution of Cooperation* offers up an answer by way of mathematics and gang members.

Around 1950, a thought-experiment called *The Prisoner's Dilemma* was invented. Here's the hypothetical: you and a fellow gang member have been captured by the police, and you have been placed in separate holding cells. The good news is, they only have enough evidence to get you on a minor charge. You're both looking at one year in prison.

A detective comes to you with an offer. Squeal on your buddy and you walk free. The downside is, your buddy gets three years because of your testimony. Do you remain loyal or do you defect?

Oh, and there's a catch. He's being given the same offer and you aren't allowed to know his decision until you make yours.

Let's think about this. If only one talks, the other gets three years. If you both squeal, you'll each get two years. If you both keep your traps shut, you'll both do a year. What do you do?

Your first thought is to remain loyal. No one wants to be a snitch. They got nothing on us. We'll each do a year and then we'll get on with our lives. But wait, what if he isn't thinking the same thing? What if he rats you out? Maybe you should protect yourself by defecting. But if you defect and he remains loyal, you'll feel horribly guilty about sending him away for three years instead of one. Besides, if we both defect, then we're just shooting ourselves in the foot anyway by doubling our own sentence.

Round and round it goes.

Which strategy is more effective? Which one gives you the best chance of a reduced sentence?

In this scenario, the harsh reality is that defecting wins. It's just simple math. If you remain loyal, then they can either defect (giving you three years) or remain loyal (giving you one year). That's an average of two years. However, by defecting, you reduce your average hard time by half: two years when they also defect, and zero when they don't. It averages out to one year.

This echoes Grant's earlier statement, "Being a giver is not good for a 100-yard dash."

This is about survival of the fittest. This is about choosing the strategy that gives you the best chance of throwing your genes as far into the future as humanly possible. Fortunately, takers don't get the last word. Fortunately, life isn't a 100-yard dash. Axelrod and Hamilton tweaked the prisoner's dilemma to better mirror the marathon of real life.

They added more rounds.

How many more rounds?

Dunno.

Which is actually brilliant. In business and in life, we never know how many rounds there will be. We never know when we're going to run into someone again. We never know whether the person we step on during our rise to the top will have the power later to drag us back down. It's Aesop's mouse who returned the kindness of the lion by gnawing off the ropes that ensnare him. It's karma, baby.

Now the problem is exponentially more difficult. Axelrod invited all the greatest minds in game theory into a tournament. The goal was to see who could come up with the best strategy to win at an undisclosed number of prisoner's dilemma rounds. Dozens of complex algorithms were written into software programs, and they were pitted against one another in head-to-head computer simulations.

The winning strategy?

Four little lines of code submitted by a Russian-born mathematical psychologist, Anatol Rapoport.

Well, winning might be a bit too strong a term. Rapoport's program actually lost more often than it won. After all, a dilemma is, by definition, two bad alternatives. If you're stuck between a rock and a hard place, then taking the lesser of two evils is a victory. The reason Rapoport's program still managed to come out on top is because it lost *less* than every other program. While the other contenders were taking huge losses, Rapoport's program was able to minimize the damages.

Before you get ahead of me, the best strategy wasn't to simply always remain loyal. Do the right thing! Stay true to your friends, no matter what! Honor among thieves! Turn the other cheek! Yeah, those programs got trounced by self-serving, dynamically-learning programs that picked up the pattern and exploited it. In other words, the doormats got walked over. The "givers" ended up at the bottom of the pile, just like the results of Adam Grant's research.

The best strategy wasn't to defect every time, either. You might think that it would stand to reason that squealing like a pig would be a smart place to start for any program whose goal was self-preservation. After all, in an individual game, defecting is the mathematically wise choice. Why wouldn't you just do that over and over until the tournament was done?

Because the other programs also picked up on that pattern and defected right back, racking up jail time for both sides in the process. A few battles were won, but the war was lost. We're talking heavy casualties.

Back and forth they went, trying to find the perfect balance between loyalty and defection. Meanwhile each coder cracked the other program's code and picked apart its weaknesses.

Still, no one beat Rapoport's simple four-line program.

When learning about the art of mentalism, I came across a trick that would allow anyone to play against a dozen chess grandmasters at once…blindfolded (using audible chess notation only.) Of course, you'll lose a few of the games. After all, these are grandmasters—the best in the world—and you likely had a social life at some point. Oh, and you'll also be blindfolded. But you'll also play some games to a draw, and even win a few others! In fact, as a whole, the group will not beat you.

From the outside, it appears that only a genius could complete this feat. Or perhaps a highly sophisticated chess-playing computer program. But keep in mind, *anyone* can do this. What appears incredibly complex is actually quite simple; even more simple than a four-line computer program.

The first grandmaster is playing white. Their move is made and you remember it. You move to the next table and play it against the second grandmaster, who is playing black. They, in turn will respond (audibly, of course) and you'll remember their move, playing it against grandmaster number one when you get all the way back around to the first table. The pattern continues like this until all the games are over. What's really happening is the grandmasters are playing chess against *each other*. All you have to do? Whatever the last guy did.

If you wanted to make it more deceptive, you'd change up the pairs so that it wouldn't be as obvious. For example, you might play table one against table eight and table two against table five, etc. It requires a bit of memorization skill, but absolutely zero chess grandmastery on your part. The blindfold is a nice touch though, isn't it?

Just do what the other guy did...that's the secret. It's simple and incredibly effective.

That's the same secret as Rapoport's program. Do what the other guy did. If he cooperated on the previous round, you cooperate on the next round. If he threw you under the bus, then you throw him under the bus. Simple.

But what do you do on the first round? We won't know what the other guy did until the next round.

The answer? Cooperate. Start by treating your partner as you would like to be treated.

Besides the golden rule, there are many other ethical qualities to this program. First, it's trustworthy. Very soon, the other program will pick up on the pattern and know exactly what to expect from you. No games, no subterfuge, no hidden agendas. Just genuine and consistent. Second, it's forgiving. If a defector changes his ways and cooperates, then you immediately cooperate again. The other cheek is turned and you willingly make yourself vulnerable to another defection. No jealousy and no passive-aggressive punishment.

But the program also protects itself. If they defect, you defect right back. Once. The punishment fits the crime. It's tit for tat. In fact, that's what Rapoport called it: "Tit for Tat". Axelrod ran his tournaments in subsequent years, and Tit for Tat has again come out on top. It is the program to beat. It loses almost every battle, but it wins the war.

In the cut-throat, competitive prisoner's dilemma tournament that Axelrod created, it is survival of the fittest. What makes you fit to win? The same qualities that make you fit to be called a "good person". Coincidence? Doubt it.

Again, it's Grant's givers who end up at the top.

In a short-term sprint, it does pay to lie, cheat, and steal. However, the important things in life aren't won by a series of unrelated short-term sprints. The important things in life are about the long-term marathon. In a marathon, the tortoise beats the hare. In influence, the ethical beats the easy.

BECOME MORE INFLUENTIAL: YOUR NEXT STEP

Throughout this book, we've peeled back the onion layers of the T.R.U.E. Hierarchy of Influence. We've seen how adding a relationship focus to your strong communication technique increases your chances of creating influence. We've seen how higher levels of understanding gives you an advantage in all your interactions. Finally, we've explored how conducting yourself ethically boosts not only your personal integrity, but also your interpersonal influence. We've learned that influence isn't just something you *do*, it's also something you *have*.

Like most primates, we are wired to look to alphas to help us find our way when things get difficult, scary, or confusing. In a way, we want to be influenced. We are also wired to help show those below us on the totem pole the lay of the land. Influence has been a natural and necessary process for thousands of years, and it certainly isn't going away any time soon.

If you feel that you can't be influential because you aren't wired like an alpha, you don't have a powerful title, or because you don't have a large network, then don't worry. Real influence was never about those things anyway. Real influence is available to anyone.

So is my email newsletter. I'd love to periodically send you short but awesome emails that will help you to connect and build more influence.

These simple, science-based strategies have helped managers, leaders, salespeople, and entrepreneurs turn frustrating interactions into moments of real and lasting influence. You'll look forward to these emails, I promise.

If you're ready for more on the science of human connection and influence, then visit the link below right now and type in your email address.

www.MoreInfluential.com

DID YOU ENJOY THE BOOK?

The single best thing you can do to support an author is leave an honest review of their book on websites like Amazon, Barnes and Noble, and GoodReads.

Please visit www.MoreInfluential.com/review and leave one or more reviews using the links provided.

Thanks in advance! :-)

ACKNOWLEDGEMENTS

I'd like to say thanks.

TO MY SUPPORT SYSTEM

Katie, Chloe, Sophie, Max, Mom, Dad, Chris, Marianne, Ray, Rick, Jane, Audrey, Meg, James, and all my aunts, uncles, and cousins. Over the years you've picked cards, made introductions, clicked my links, taken my surveys, watched my videos, shared my articles, and read my books. You've also watched kids, cooked food, and swung hammers for me. If you're not sick of me by now, you'll never be. For that, I'm truly grateful. I really enjoy doing life alongside all of you.

TO THE PEOPLE RESPONSIBLE

To my repeat-offender editor Jeanette Shaw, my eagle-eyed, uber punctual, (and uber punctuational) "grammar Nazi" Melissa Caminneci, my book-interior-prettier-upper Phillip Gessert, my cover designer Avanska, my agent Giles Anderson, and my long-time photographer Bob Bartlett. (P.S. Don't blame Melissa for the grammar in this section. This is all me.) Let's do this again some-time!

TO MY AMAZING LAUNCH TEAM

Katie Pereira, Karen Bessette, Gregory Dwyer, Ken Campbell, Jason Bradley, Dan Gushue, Kathy Roberts, Taw Pruitt, David Hooper, Tom Cutts, Aimee Bridgwood, Timothy Nickerson, Chris Wood, Alese Morgan, Deborah Luce, Carole Pepe, Perry Carpenter, Daniel Chard, Guy D. Alba, Julie Meadows DiDonna, Erin Ray, Rod Thorell, Kyle Peron, Sally Herndon, Joe Fingerhut, Marianne Morin, Scott Barhold, Rachel Stevenson, Costas Peppas, David Pereira, Amanda Briggs, Jorge Santana, Scott Shapland, David M. Frees, Ted Peterson, Bro Gilbert, Derek Heron, Ray Engan, Kathy Coval, David DeHerrera, Kate Reilly, Chantia Johns, Sean Magee, Jodie Madore, Briceston Anderson, Ed Fox, Josh Fletcher, Mike Toy, Bruce Hunt, Bruce Robinson, Silvia Collins-Brown, Katie Carrier, Julia Eleftheriou, Jessica Teixeira, Mark Shaughnessy, John Kline, Sixto Carlos, Mark Corona, Yvonne Hernandez, David Bilan, Gerald Velazquez, John Kaplan, Micke Askernäs, Chong Beng Lim, Sean Jacob, Michael Glowacki, Martin Duffy, Annabelle Hohmann, Joel Schultz, Jeffrey Richards, Karylle Allick, David Black, Ali Said Jamal Eddine, and Adrienne Krouskop. You suffered through bad drafts of the manuscript, offered invaluable feedback, and made this book much, much better in the process. You also championed its release, shared every last promotional piece on social media, and encouraged me through the tough spots. Your contributions cannot be overstated.

TO THE INFLUENCERS

Paul Hughes, Sharí Alexander, Rich Testa, Officer David Godin, Howard Tiegel, Justin Cook, Emily Lyons, Gavin Cresswell, Chris Maccaro, Don Pazour, Dan de Grandpre, Ora Shtull, Dr. Robert

Cialdini, Chris Brogan, Yu-Kai Chou, Roger Dooley, Dan Ariely, Tom Neilssen, Tom Schwab, David Hooper, Thor Conklin, Chris Voss, Nir Eyal, David Newman, Tiffani Bova, Joel Comm, Ron Friedman, Shawn Ellis, Barry Friedman, Alan Siegel, Jeff Shore, Erik Qualman, Jamie Turner, Tamsen Webster, Deborah Gardner, Lolly Daskal, Marc Jaillet, and Tim Grahl. You've inspired me with your stories, coached me, advocated for me, and impressed me. Thanks for being influential the *right* way. I'd follow any one of you anywhere.

TO MY EARLIEST THUNDERCLAP SUPPORTERS (IN CHRONOLOGICAL ORDER)

Julia Eleftheriou (who somehow supported the campaign even before I did), Kyle Peron, Adrienne Krouskop, Katie Carrier, Rod Thorell, **Perry Carpenter**, Martin Duffy, Kate Reilly, **David Deherrera**, Scott Barhold, Aimee Bridgwood, Julie Meadows DiDonna, **Yvonne Hernandez**, Ken Campbell, Karen Bessette, John J. Austrian, Bro Gilbert, **Gregory Dwyer**, Kathy Roberts, Sara Runner, Erin Ray, Bruce Hunt, Chantia Johns, Joel Comm, Briceston Anderson, David Black, Sean Jacob, Sally Herndon, Nathan McGlothlin, **Karylle Allick**, **Kate Waters**, RealMenLiveToxinFree, Paul "sabret00the," Davis_316, **Kathy Coval**, Sixto Carlos, Ron Friedman, Ph.D., Shawn Ellis, Mark Shaughnessy, Helen Andromalos, Alese Morgan, Nate Maingard, Mike Toy, Gail Elmore, Ishini Gunasekera, Deborah Luce, **David Norton**, RileySalesHVAC, **Kimberly Long**, David Hooper, Carole Pepe, **Joanne Calhoun**, John Kaplan, Taw Pruitt, Marlan "Hiliminarious", **Mohammad Parwaz**, Neil Gordon, Jenna O'Leary, Yetti O'Leary, Katie Pereira, Jane Madore, Meredith Wood, Paula Mosher Wallace, David M Frees, Brandon Ellis, George Weinstein, J.C. Stockli, Jamie Thomas, David Pereira, Kelvin Morrison, **Jamie Turner**, Chip Eichelberger, Karlo Lopez, Tim Piccirillo, Derek Heron, Joshua Seth, Robert McEntee, Cara Golson, Benjamin Budzak,

Will Baldry, Kristian Bennett, **Silvia Collins-Brown**, **Jennifer Culbreth**, Bethanie Castelnuovo, **Amanda Briggs**, Verkaufsforschung, Jessica Tomczak, Hester Lester, Jeffrey Richards, CH, **Ron Hudspeth**, Barry Friedman, Timothy Nickerson, Janice Vaughn Craft, John Silwonuk, Rob Austin, **Tim Mannix**, Daniel Perry, Richard Testa, **Celeste Atkins**, Joel Schultz, Erin Scanlon, Ely M. Pisco, Kate Zephyrhawke, Kathy Monteiro Andrews, Lesko Talks Windows, Jessi Krieg, daveOwl, Lissa Smith, Guy D. Alba, Paula Kelley, Phil Allen, The HR Engineers, Daniel Chard, Tommy Johns, Judith Mazziotti, Meghan O'Leary, Laurie Etchison, Guy Coulson, Donal O'Neill, Chris Edmondson, **Beth Edwards**, Ginny Tonic, Shelly Cahill Smith, Jocelyn Shinney, and anyone else who supported after this went off to press. Special nod to Timmy David, Amy Eddy, and Lolly Daskal for the extra Twitter love.

Those whose names appear in **bold print** *supported the campaign across multiple platforms.*

TO THOSE WORTHY OF SOME EXTRA THANKS

Ken Campbell, Rod Thorell, Adrienne Krouskop, and Tom Cutts deserve special acknowledgement for providing some of the most comprehensive, honest, and valuable feedback that I received. Although, the promised Darkwing Duck references were conspicuously absent, Ken.

Julia Eleftheriou and Joel Comm for blowing up our Thunderclap campaign overnight.

Jeff Shore, Meg Kelley, Loan Mansy, Annabelle Hohmann, Jamie Turner, and Barry Friedman for surprising me with support and encouragement that went beyond expectation.

Neil Gordon, for helping me to clarify this message.

And finally, Karen Bessette. Because she's my mom.

Hi Mom.

ABOUT THE AUTHOR

A cross between Simon Sinek and David Blaine, Tim David writes the kinds of books he likes to read. He supports his writing habit by...

SPEAKING

Tim regularly presents highly entertaining, high-content programs at conferences, meetings, and events on the importance of human connection in a digital world.

http://www.TimDavidSpeaks.com

BACKGROUND AND PERSONAL LIFE

For eight years, Tim made his living as a magician and mentalist touring the country to make people laugh and think. Shortly after starting a family, Tim switched his focus to translating the lessons he learned from show business to the world of "real" business.

HOBBIES

Besides being a neuroscience nerd and a psychology junkie, Tim can be seen on a disc golf course, a Brazilian Jiu-Jitsu mat, or being overly competitive at yard games.

Tim lives with his wife and three young children in Massachusetts.

Email: tim@moreinfluential.com Twitter: @TimDavidMagic

ALSO BY TIM DAVID

"Tim David offers keen insight into how to better connect with others in business and in life." —ADAM GRANT, Wharton professor and New York Times bestselling author of Give and Take

The Science and Secrets Behind Seven Words That Motivate, Engage, and Influence

MAGIC WORDS

TIM DAVID

MAGIC WORDS: The Science and Secrets Behind Seven Words that Motivate, Engage, and Influence (Penguin Random House)

"*Elegant and concise.*"

—*NY Times*

"*Top ten psychology book of 2016.*"

—*Blinkist Magazine*

Fans of Dr. Robert Cialdini, Daniel Pink, and Malcolm Gladwell will enjoy this in-depth look at the often surprising magic behind how words can inspire and influence others. By exploring seven "magic words," Tim David explains the important psychology behind how what we say affects those around us in business and in life. Full of startling scientific research, humorous anecdotes, and word-for-word scripts, this book will help you be a better leader, salesperson, or parent.

Available now at: **www.MagicWordsBook.com** and all major book retailers.

AVAILABLE NOW FOR FREE

THE INFLUENCE CHEAT SHEET: 61 Science-Based Sales Techniques

The more influential components your communication contains, the more likely it is to succeed. Science has uncovered some powerful techniques. If you don't know about them, then you're behind the times and losing sales.

Beginning with Robert Cialdini's six techniques from his classic book, Influence: The Psychology of Persuasion, this handy reference guide details influence techniques gathered from a wide range of psychological literature.

Visit www.MoreInfluential.com/cheatsheet to grab your free PDF copy immediately.

19 THINGS MANAGERS SHOULD NEVER SAY (But Probably Do Anyway...)

These are so common that you're probably saying at least twenty of them. After researching and writing *Magic Words* I realized there are a lot of ways to say things right, but FAR more ways to say them WRONG.

I guarantee these words and phrases are causing you to miss out on time, energy, and even money that you don't even realize you're missing out on. BOTTOM LINE: If you say these things, you're killing your influence.

Visit www.MoreInfluential.com/leadership to grab your free PDF copy immediately.